# GET WEIRD!

## 101 INNOVATIVE WAYS TO MAKE YOUR COMPANY A GREAT PLACE TO WORK

### John Putzier

AMACOM AMERICAN MANAGEMENT ASSOCIATION

New York • Atlanta • Boston • Chicago • Kansas City • San Francisco
Washington, D. C. • Brussels • Mexico City • Tokyo • Toronto

This publication is designed to provide accurate and authoritative information in regard
to the subject matter covered. It is sold with the understanding that the publisher is not
engaged in rendering legal, accounting, or other professional service. If legal advice or
other expert assistance is required, the services of a competent professional person
should be sought.

Library of Congress Cataloging-in-Publication Data

Putzier, John, 1951–
   Get Weird!: 101 innovative ways to make your company a great place to work/
John Putzier.
     p. cm.
   Includes index.
   ISBN 0-8144-7114-5 (pbk.)
   1. Organizational change—Handbooks, manuals, etc. 2. Personnel management—
Handbooks, manuals, etc. 3. Job satisfaction—Handbooks, manuals, etc. I. Title.

HD58.8 .P88 2001
658.4′02—dc21

                                                                    00-068977

Printing number
10 9

To my Mom and Dad,
Jack and Gwendolyn Putzier:
For allowing
and encouraging me
to be me.
I love you.

# CONTENTS

**PART 3  WEIRD IDEAS FOR THE CARE AND FEEDING
OF TODAY'S TALENT (aka Retention)**

**PART 4 WEIRD IDEAS FOR CHANGING YOUR COMPANY CULTURE (aka Fun & Games with a Purpose & a Profit)**

**PART 5    WEIRD IDEAS FOR PERKS, PAY, AND PATS ON THE BACK (aka Recognition & Incentives)**

## PART 6 WEIRD IDEAS FOR EDUCATING TODAY'S TALENT
### (aka Training & Development)

**PART 8 WHERE'S 101? (aka It's All In Your Head!)**

# ACKNOWLEDGMENTS

It's really difficult to figure out whom to acknowledge for my being able to write this book. After all, I wrote it! However, I do want to thank my parents, Jack and Gwen Putzier, for making me so weird. Most kids would probably sue their parents for such a thing, but I am grateful. I think many so-called normal parents raise some pretty weird kids, so I am glad I had weird parents so that I wound up better than normal. Is that weird? (You will see later in the book why it's so wonderful to be weird.)

I also want to thank my lovely and literate wife, Loriann, for allowing, supporting, and continuing to encourage my weirdness. In fact, she is an active participant. She actually married me because of my weirdness. As my editor-in-chief (in life), she also has a knack for brutal honesty (aka tough love), which all weird writers and husbands need. They don't like it, but they need it. Loriann exemplifies the concept of unconditional love, and I love her for it.

And of course no parent could survive without a critique from the kid(s). Seriously, my son Nathan John is truly a blessing; he is always an invaluable resource and is always supportive and respectful to me and to Loriann without ever having to be asked (an extremely rare trait in kids today). Nate keeps me grounded and is quite the analytical type, which I am not. He sees things I cannot, has fresh and intelligent insights, and is almost always right. Just ask him!

I would also like to thank my literary agent, Mark Ryan of New Brand Agency Group. If it weren't for Mark's skill, passion, and patience, you probably would not be reading this right now. Mark was the first agent who called me with both an excitement in his voice and an "out-of-the-box" approach to life, two things that made all the difference to me.

Speaking of patience, no one had to be more patient than Adrienne Hickey, executive editor of AMACOM Books. When I talk about the experience of writing a book and working with a major publisher, I often use the analogy of what it would be like for a woman to endure a long, painful delivery of her first child and name him, then give him up for adoption to someone who gives him a new name and takes over the process of nurturing and development.

That is the reality of being an author, and Adrienne bore the brunt of much of my pain with me. There were times when I know she was in as much pain as I, but she not only talked me through it, but also saw to it that we came through on the other side with a beautiful baby. Thank you, Adrienne, for the tough love that I (and our book) needed.

Now that I have lived through the process and can appreciate what goes into it, I must also thank Jim Bessent, AMACOM associate editor, and his team for the incredible amount of tedious work that went into wordsmithing and polishing the final manuscript. Jim was wonderful to work with, kept his sense of humor under fire, and had the patience of Job. I just hope that he and his department can now find a way to use some of the stress reliever ideas in this book.

I would be seriously remiss if I did not acknowledge the support and camaraderie of the Society for Human Resource Management (SHRM). To list everyone who has influenced and encouraged me over the years at SHRM would be impossible. However, it is noteworthy that during the placement process SHRM also expressed interest in publishing *Get Weird!* And as an example of their unconditional support and professionalism, even after my decision to go with AMACOM, they continued to support and encourage me as an author.

In particular, Laura Lawson, Manager of Book Publishing at SHRM, actually became a "voice of reason" for me when I struggled with the usual author anxiety issues, and kept reminding me that everything would be fine in the end; and it was. To all of you other SHRMers, who know who they are, I can only thank you when I see you at a future conference or some other gathering of one of the best professional organizations on the planet.

And last, so you can get on with the book, I would like to thank all my past jerk employers who tried to stifle my weirdness and created the fire in my belly to succeed as a self-unemployed consultant and speaker for these many years, just so I wouldn't have to go back to work for one of them again. A little history is important here, so you can appreciate from whence I come.

It all began with one of my first jobs, as a grocery store clerk in the 1960s. We ran out of milk, and the assistant manager asked me to put a sign in the cooler. Realizing that milk is a staple item and that customers would not be happy about this, I went into action. I went to the stock room, got a grease pencil and some poster board, and put my creativity to work. I drew a picture of a cow, spread-eagle on its back with udders hanging down, and the caption, "Sorry, but our cow died."

Customers were chuckling and commenting to one another in the cashier's line (they weren't mad!). This led the assistant manager to investigate, and the rest is history. He came back from the milk cooler, told me to take off my apron, and said, "Punch out; you're fired!" (By the way, the union did nothing to get me back.) I've been punched out ever since. The bottom line is, if I hadn't lived and worked in the world of this kind of boss for many more years after that incident, I wouldn't have needed or been able to write this book. My biggest motivator is to never have a real job again. I can say anything I want to about these people, because I doubt that they will ever read this book, and even if they do, I'll never be going back to work for any of them again anyway. Especially if you would just buy a few more copies of my book!

Vive la Weirdness!

# INTRODUCTION

Whatever happened to the good old days when employees just showed up, shut up, and did what they were told? All they ever expected was a cheesy gold watch after thirty or so years when they just couldn't do it anymore. Where I come from, that was called the "work ethic." It was a thing to be admired and revered.

News flash: It's dead! And before you start mourning, I think you might want to have a party instead. If the work ethic wasn't dead, I believe a mercy killing would be in order. Just take a look at Webster's synonyms for work: labor, travail, toil, drudgery, grind…. Hats off to all our ancestors who were willing and able to make the sacrifices necessary to afford us the luxury of working to live, instead of living to work.

With an economy that now values brains over brawn, mind over muscle, the old definitions for work and success have been turned upside down. The world of work is changing. Those changes are coming rapidly and dramatically, and they are only just beginning—24/7, flex-place, flex-time, flex-life, free agents, contingent workers, virtual employees, dot.coms out the wazoo, portable careers, Internet everything. A new language, a new lifestyle, and a new workplace are emerging and redefining the employee-employer relationship. Entering this brave new world of work is the only option left for organizations if they are to survive and succeed in this age of revolutionary change.

This book is not deep. It is, however, quite wide. It is also not long. But it is long on content. These are not apologies, but clarifications of its purpose and its value. Having attended and addressed hundreds of seminars and professional conferences of all kinds, I have constantly heard people say, and have even said myself, "If I can just get a couple of good ideas from this that I can take back and use at work, it will have been worth it."

If this is true, and if you consider how much one can invest in such conferences (registrations, airfare, rental cars, lodging, meals, lost time, etc.), you should be delighted at the return on your investment in this book. In that same spirit, I have also come to realize that time is a highly valued commodity today. Therefore, you will not have to wade through any wasted words to get the point. If an idea needs only a paragraph or two for you to get the gist, that's all there is.

The bottom line is this: *Working adults just want answers.* They want solutions to problems. Cut through the theory, skip the history lesson, save the sales pitch, and just tell me something new and practical that I can use. Give me something that works. Give me an idea that I can implement tomorrow without spending a fortune or having to get tons of committee approvals. That is what this book is designed to do.

Management consultants, trainers, and speakers learn as much from their clients as those clients learn from them. That's not a sin; it's just plain smart. If we don't learn as we go, our value to our clients diminishes. After a while, however, we tend to adopt more and more of our clients' success stories, and then we leverage them and package them as accumulated wisdom to impress future prospects and clients, who teach us even more…and the beat goes on! It has been said that "a consultant is someone who borrows your watch to tell you what time it is; and then keeps your watch." This book is my attempt to return some of those watches.

Professional speakers, trainers, and consultants are also messengers of success (their own and others'), and this book includes some of the best ideas and practices that I have seen work in just about every industry or profession imaginable over the years. Some of the other ideas are original, untested personal brainspurts (you'll get a definition of what a brainspurt is in Part 1) that may have never been used but that are certainly worth tweaking, trying, and sharing.

For those of you who are as old as I (that's none of your business), I think you will agree that few, if any, of us would have had the chutzpa or the stupidity to recommend some of these crazy ideas back in the 1970s or 1980s, or even the early 1990s. We would have been quickly ostracized or been the unfortunate recipients of out-placement, a reduction in force, a downsizing, a rightsizing, or some other corporate euphemism for "You're fired!"

Yes, we may have wanted to recommend these ideas, but until now, most employers have been in the driver's seat for eons. Today, the situation can best be seen graphically in the ancient symbol of the yin/yang.

My fellow old closet hippies probably know this already, but one of the concepts that the yin/yang represents is the coming together of opposing forces, such as life and death, man and woman, black and white, and so on. Another well-known tenet of this Eastern philosophy of opposing forces is that in every crisis there is an opportunity (more specifically, the Chinese say that "Crisis is opportunity riding a dangerous horse").

So why do I bring this up now? Because the current prolonged skilled labor *crisis* has finally created the *opportunity* (born out of the necessity) for employers to try almost anything to attract, retain, and motivate the best and the brightest. Employers are no longer in the driver's seat, and that can be good news for everyone.

The recent and current trends toward making workplaces more fun, more flexible, and more compatible with different peoples and lifestyles isn't happening because a whole bunch of bosses suddenly woke up one day born again and hell bent on creating more benevolent organizations. They had to open their minds and their wallets if they wanted to stay in business.

A perfect, bellwether case in point is the advent of domestic partner benefits, i.e., life, health, and other benefits for same-sex partners of employees (also known as "spousal equivalents"). The introduction of domestic partner benefits was one of the first and most significant *major* changes (and a sign of things to come) to be introduced into the traditional corporate value system, and it has now become an accepted practice in many organizations with a high demand for highly skilled workers. It was a turning point in the field of human resource management, and there is no turning back now.

The bottom line is that this prolonged talent shortage *crisis* is the most significant *opportunity* for you to revolutionize your world of human resources since they started being called human resources. Who cares if it isn't rooted in benevolence? Just ride this dangerous horse into the brave new world of work!

This skilled talent shortage is not just a result of a business cycle. It is predicted to last well into the twenty-first century, requiring companies to go to extremes to attract and hold onto employees. According to a year-long study conducted by a team from McKinsey & Co. (a study involving seventy-seven companies and almost 6,000 managers and executives), "the most important corporate resource over the next twenty years will be talent: smart, sophisticated business people who are technologically literate, globally astute, and operationally agile."

To further quote McKinsey, in their report "The War for Talent," "the search for the best and the brightest will become a constant, costly battle, a fight with no final victory. Not only will companies have to devise more imaginative hiring practices; they will also have to work harder to keep their best people."

It used to be that small companies tried to emulate the big boys (the large, old, established organizations) and tried to model their growth strategies after them. But today, big companies are trying to act small. They are now competing against start-ups and entrepreneurial companies where people have lots of "elbow room" (multifunctional responsibility), lots of "head room" (where they can make decisions on their own, without having to battle a bureaucracy), and the potential to make lots of money!

As a career human resources practitioner and consultant, I must offer this caveat about using the ideas in this book to change your company. These ideas should not be mere add-ons to your existing operations. If they are to make a real difference in your company, you have to adopt them as an essential element of the way you do business. Do not become a member of the "program/idea of the month" club. If you want your company to be outstanding, you must be willing and able to stand out. I have seen too many companies that want the benefits of seeming to be different, without the risks that come with actually being different. Make it a mindset, not a program.

You may scoff at some of these ideas and say *aha!* at others. And you shouldn't expect to use every idea, any more than you would expect to use every concept you hear at a conference. Some are industry-specific; others are more universal. However, I do suggest that you abandon your traditional industry or professional perspective when reading this book because many truly creative ideas come from places you have not looked in the past.

You will also discover that this is much more than just a reference book. Part 1 introduces you to the creative thinking and problem-solving process and is put there to give you some of the tools and techniques that were actually used to discover and develop a lot of the ideas in this book. Think of them as ideas for getting ideas. If you read these tricks and techniques first, and practice them as you go, you will find yourself tweaking and enhancing the ideas in the later parts, and then you will start getting your own original ideas, which I want for my next book. I want my watches back!

Since I am a staunch believer in incentives and pay for performance, I am offering you an opportunity to capitalize on your new-found creativity by submitting your own ideas for possible inclusion in a future publication. Specifically, Idea #101 will be your own. If your idea is good enough for inclusion in any future manuscript I submit for publication, you will receive a free, autographed copy of *Get Weird!*

Finally, it is important that you understand the theme of weirdoes and weirdness. Normal people may take these words the wrong way. A weirdo is anybody who is not like you. That's why there are so many of them out there. To "get weird" is to "be yourself," sometimes at the expense of how others may see you. To quote Arno Penzias, who won the Nobel Prize in physics (for discovering staticlike radiation that provided watershed evidence of the Big Bang), "If you are a truly creative person, you know that feeling insecure and lonely is par for the course. You can't have it both ways. You can't be creative, and conform too. You have to recognize that what makes you different also makes you creative."

Thus, people who excel in a particular field or area of expertise, or who are very high-level thinkers in a given subject, can appear "weird" to the rest of the world, and vice versa. Weirdness is a two-way street. Understanding the concepts of weirdoes and weirdness is tantamount to understanding diversity to the max. It is the synergy (yin and yang) of high performance and individuality.

Another way to understand and advance this mindset is to abandon the concept of society and its organizations as a melting pot, which is a term rooted in the advent of the Industrial Revolution. What does a melting pot represent? It represents all different types of people brought together, heated up, and melted into an indistinguishable amalgam.

A better analogy for today would be to think of us as a stir-fry, or a tossed salad. Can you see the difference? You would never put the vegetables and the meat and all the other ingredients into a blender and turn them into a liquid blob, would you? Of course not. You still have all the different ingredients, but each one continues to maintain its individuality (flavor) while enhancing the overall experience. You can still taste the tomato.

In Part 1, "Tapping Your Natural Weirdness," you will be introduced to some of these concepts and, I hope, will learn that being a weirdo and being able to tap your natural weirdness are both wonderful things for which to strive. In the remainder of the book, you'll find innovative ideas that result from the fearless creativity of people who have embraced weirdness and used it to make their companies great places in which to work.

So fasten your seatbelt, unzip your forehead, and welcome to a brave new world of weird ideas!

# TAPPING YOUR NATURAL WEIRDNESS

## aka CREATIVE THINKING & PROBLEM SOLVING

*There's a famous line from Eleanor Roosevelt that goes, "Great minds discuss ideas; average minds discuss events; small minds discuss people." Before we get into the actual ideas for changing the world of work, it will behoove you to learn a little about how you can use your own great mind to embark on a journey of great ideas.*

*Tapping your natural weirdness means becoming more of what you already were. Are you confused yet? Bear in mind that the older we get, the less creative and open-minded we become. Also bear in mind that this is the result not of aging, but of conditioning. Want proof?*

*Back in the early days of the Head Start program, 1,600 children were tested on a number of things, one of them being "divergent thinking," i.e., thinking outside the box.*

*At ages 3 to 5, 98 percent scored in the genius category for divergent thinking. Five years later (ages 8 to 10), this number had plummeted to only 32 percent. Senility already? Five years later again (ages 13 to 15), it was down to 10 percent. More than 200,000 adults over age 25 were given the same test, and only 2 percent scored in the genius category (and they were probably unemployable).*

*As you will discover, the barriers to creativity and innovation develop over time, which is why many forms of therapy include some form of regression to our childhood. Most of our problems develop over time, and we need to strip away the barnacles to find our true self again, i.e., "to tap our natural weirdness."*

*Note that creativity and innovation are not the same thing. Simply put, creativity is the act of coming up with a new idea or a new twist on an old idea. It does not imply action, just thought and discovery. Innovation, on the other hand, requires action. It requires follow-through. It implies implementation, which is what the world pays for. This section gives you tips and techniques for generating new and unusual ideas, but if you plan to get paid for your ideas, you must do something with them.*

## Three Barriers to Creativity

There are three common barriers to maximizing your creativity (i.e., tapping your natural weirdness): (1) structures and patterns, (2) judgmentalism, and (3) resistance to change. And all three of these barriers are rooted in a common desire to stay within our comfort zones.

### STRUCTURES AND PATTERNS

About 85 percent of the average adult's day is habit. Structures and patterns are our habits, our way of designing predictability and stability into our lives. We develop our personal routines so that we can operate in mental cruise control. It's comfortable.

For example, we get up every morning at about the same time; we probably turn on our favorite radio or television station; we go through our "morning routine"; we take the same route to work every day, with our favorite morning station on the car stereo; we see the same people, do the same job, go home (same route, same radio station as yesterday), go through our evening routine, maybe watch our favorite TV shows, and go to bed. There's no need to change the alarm. It will be the same tomorrow. And so on, and so on, and so on.... That is what I call mental cruise control, or personal autopilot!

Have you ever driven to work and not even remembered doing it? I think you have, because I've been behind you! The point is, if you do something the same way every day and see the same things every day, you eventually don't even have to think about it. Comfortable, but boring!

## JUDGMENTALISM

The second barrier, judgmentalism, has to do with our decision-making comfort zone. Adults have to make so many decisions every day, and have to deal with so many unknowns, that it is nice to have some decisions already made...permanently! This includes your "decisions" on what is right and wrong, good and bad, normal and weird. These decisions could be related to social issues, religious issues, political issues, or any other issues that you have the right to make decisions about and stick to, come hell or high water.

Once we are comfortable with our judgments, we tend to associate with others who generally agree with us, join organizations that are consistent with our way of thinking, and proceed to judge the rest of the world through our collectively myopic, self-righteous eyes. Comfortable, but stupid!

How does this happen? One way to understand judgmentalism is to think of your brain as a filing cabinet. When a piece of mail or other information crosses your desk, do you always file it away? Of course not. Before you decide to file something away in your filing cabinet, literal or cranial, the information must pass through a buffer system. And each buffer in this system requires you to make a judgment call.

You are doing it right now. Subconsciously, you are saying to yourself, "Do I believe this stuff?" This is the buffer of *truth*. If you do not believe something, you are probably not going to bother filing it away for later reference. Unfortunately, our judgment call as to what is believable is influenced by what we *want* to believe and can therefore be erroneous.

## *This is Your Brain...*

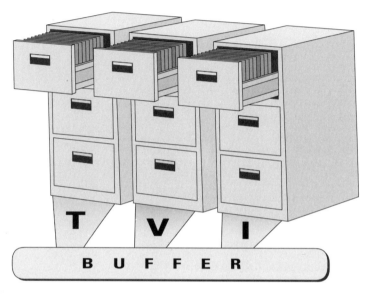

**Figure 1–1**

If information makes it past your buffer of truth, it must then pass through your buffer of *value*—the "Do I care?" buffer. Do I want to save this information for future retrieval? Do I, or will I, have any need for it? You may say to yourself, "I don't need to remember this. I already know what these people (this issue, this organization) are (is) about." And, once again, judgmentalism takes place.

Finally, if information passes the buffers of truth and value, it must then be categorized. This is your *indexing* buffer. These are the little Pendaflex™ tabs in your head that organize information.

If you've had your filing cabinet for many years, and a piece of information comes across your desk that you decide to save, but that doesn't quite fit your existing, well-established filing system, do you reorganize your filing system? It's doubtful. Either you don't file the piece of information or you misfile it in a folder that is "close enough." Again, judgmentalism takes place—in this case, through your personal paradigm of where the information should fit.

The older we get, the more files we have created, and the more we hate to create new files. It's more comfortable to force the world of information into our established system of thinking. And that is judgmentalism.

### RESISTANCE TO CHANGE

Finally comes resistance to change. This barrier is very much an outgrowth of the other two. The more structured and patterned you are, the more you want to stay within those routines or habits. The more judgmental you are, the more committed to your established thoughts and opinions you become. And, as with the first two barriers, resistance to change is also an attempt to stay within our personal comfort zones.

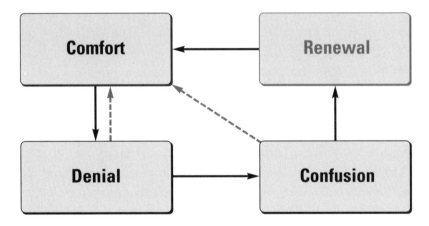

Figure 1–2

We all go through a predictable series of emotions when faced with a change of any kind, with the primary objective, whether conscious or not, of getting back to our comfort zones as soon as possible. In fact, many people never make it all the way around the cycle because of the constant pull to get back to their comfort zone. In other words, they slide back to square one to avoid working through these other emotions (thus, the dotted lines) and never accomplish the change.

As an example, I think of the time when I bought my first computer. I had been in business for a couple of years, and I always took my program materials to a local copy shop. I paid a young woman there on an hourly basis to put my typewritten pages and scribbles into an acceptable format, using a common word processing program. Then I would drive back to the copy shop, pick up what she had done, take it back to the office, proof it, change it, and drive back to the copy shop to have the revisions made, usually repeating this process several times.

In the meantime, a friend of mine had purchased his first Macintosh computer and kept telling me that I should get one. I was comfortably in denial. I rationalized that I did not have time to learn how to use a computer, that computers were expensive, that the way I was doing it was working just fine, yada yada yada. Then at year end, when I was doing my taxes, I saw how much I had spent on word processing services. I could have bought several computers and personal training to boot!

So, I took the giant leap out of denial, bought a *used* Mac (because I still wasn't sure I was really going to commit to this), and booted it up. Yikes! What is this? I knew it was a mistake. I should have listened to myself when I was still in my comfort zone.

I called technical support. The help desk guy asked me what kind of computer I had. I said it was beige. He said that it appeared that I had a pebcac problem. Another techie acronym! What's a pebcac problem? "Problem Exists Between Computer And Chair." Cute!

To make a long story short, I eventually not only learned how wonderful (and cost-effective) it was to design my own materials, but started preaching to others about why they should have a computer. I was a born-again computer geek. Renewal! But, before I knew it, I was right back in my comfort zone. Here comes a notice of a software upgrade. I don't need the newest version of word processing software! Version 0.01 works fine for me! And here we go again. Back to denial. Anything to stay comfortable.

This is the purpose of the "Challenges for Change" section in this part. This section is intended to help you change your thinking about change itself. You have to literally practice introducing safe, incremental changes in your personal life in order to start becoming comfortable with change, and ultimately seeking it out on your own. You must get out of the habit of getting into habits.

Every change management guru says that change is stressful. And stress is *always* rooted in a perceived loss of control. If you are not in control of change, you will be stressed. Pretty simple. Here's a bonus idea for you: Why not quit being the victim of change (i.e., always having to respond to others' ideas) and start initiating it yourself? If you are the one initiating change, you are no longer the victim. Let the rest of the world be stressed!

Now, let's get weird!

## Second Right Answers

Most people get paid to solve problems. If there were no problems, they wouldn't need you. However, in our daily quest to solve as many problems as possible, we tend to focus more on the quantity of solutions than on their quality or creativity. After all, doesn't it feel good to scratch those things off your to-do list?

As a result, most people jump on the first, and usually the most obvious, solution to a problem. This behavior is a result of past conditioning to get the "right" answer. Very seldom was there a second right answer in school. That's not how you got the best grade. Believe me, I know. We just aren't conditioned to reject an apparently obvious solution in the quest for a different one. Most organizations also tend to reward fast solutions over creative ones, even though they would prefer to have both.

The "Second Right Answer" requires you to take a "time-out" after discovering the first solution and press forward for additional solutions. When you do so, you will almost always discover that the second or even the third, fourth, or fifth right answer is more innovative, cost-effective, or enduring than most first right answers ever are.

For example, during a customer service consulting assignment with a major oil company, one of the objectives was to increase the volume of full-service business, which is much more profitable. As part of that objective, the company wanted the service station attendants to get to know the full-service customers, greet them by name, and remember their names in future transactions, i.e., engage in relationship selling.

Fortunately, almost all full-service customers use some form of credit card, so the customer's name is readily available. The challenge, though, was to get high school–age, minimum-wage employees to learn the customers' names, remember them, and recognize those customers in the future. As you can imagine, these employees were not the least bit interested in developing relationships with their customers; particularly at minimum wage. And even if they were willing, it's not an easy thing to do.

The first right answer (i.e., the consultant's) was to send all the station attendants to training on the importance of customer service and relationship building, and ultimately to a memory development course on how to remember people's names. However, because of the large number of people in these positions, their geographic dispersion, and the high turnover in the job, this was just not feasible, nor was it affordable. Too bad for the consultant!

So, moving on to the second right answer, we asked the question: "Is there anyone out there already doing this successfully?" The answer was yes, The next questions were who, where, and how?

There was a young man at one of the service stations who remembered his customers' names after only one transaction. After one transaction, he could greet customers by name without ever seeing the credit card again. He would go straight to the gas cap, and while he was removing it and beginning the filling process, he would say, "Good morning, Mr. Jones." As the tank was filling, he would go to the customer's window and take his credit card to process the transaction, thus saving the customer's time. How did he do it? Was he a memory expert? No. He had found the second right answer, and it was *simply* amazing. Here it is: Whenever a customer pulled into the full-service lane, he would take the credit card, read the customer's name, write it on a piece of masking tape, and stick the tape on the gas cap! Then, the next time that customer came in, he didn't even need to see the credit card. He would remove the gas cap, glance at it, see that it said Mr. Jones, and say, "Good morning, Mr. Jones. How are you today?"

He said, "These customers will never catch on to the trick, because full-service customers never see their own gas cap." For the cost of a couple of rolls of masking tape, every gas station attendant in the country could "develop a relationship" with every full-service customer he or she had.

Here's another one. There was a little "mom and pop" pizza shop that was threatened when a large, national franchise store came to town and started running huge ads in the local phone book. Since the mom and pop shop couldn't afford the first right answer of running equally large ads, out of necessity it had to look for another solution.

So, the shop ran a promotion. *Bring us our competition's ad out of your phone book and get two pizzas for the price of one!* The competition's advertising became the shop's promotional coupon. This was perfectly legal because people can do whatever they want to with their copy of the phone book. Unfortunately (ha ha), many people also stole the ads out of phone books in phone booths and other public places. While the mom and pop store's sales went through the roof, the competitor's advertising was disappearing at the same time.

Mom and pop also benefited from another common effect of the second right answer. The local media got wind of it and turned it into the quintessential David and Goliath story. You can imagine the result of that free publicity. The entire community rallied around the little guys and essentially ran the big guy out of town.

There are limitless examples of how second right answers have been used successfully. It just takes a little self-discipline to press on after you find the first right answer. Although it may seem to take longer than the first right answer, which it does at first, the quality and payback of these solutions more than make up for it. Just compare the cost-benefit of the examples above if you want proof.

## In Search of QWERTYUIOPs

What the heck is a QWERTYUIOP? Have you ever used a typewriter or computer keyboard? Right! It's the top row of keys on your keyboard. Now, if you were to design a computer or typewriter keyboard for the first time, today, what do you think the probability is that you would arrange the keys in this manner? Zero, unless you're a masochist.

You might be surprised to learn that this was not the sequence of letters that appeared on the first typewriters in the 1800s. At one point, the typists were typing faster than the technology could handle, and the keys kept jamming. As an interim solution, the engineers rearranged the keys into an illogical sequence to slow down the typists until a better solution could be found. By the time the engineers had developed an improved mechanism, the typists had learned the new sequence of keys and did not want the discomfort of "unlearning" again.

The bottom line is, here we are, more than a hundred years later, still using an illogical, inefficient system because that's the way we've always done it, and we don't want to learn something new. There's that comfort zone thing again!

"In Search of QWERTYUIOPs" is symbolic of things that are illogical, outdated, or inefficient, but that have never been challenged or changed because "that's the way we've always done it." These things could be policies, procedures, meetings, committees, reports, or any other activity that saps time, money, or energy from the organization.

For example, during my years working in a very large corporation, we had to submit weekly reports by Friday at 2 P.M., monthly reports by the second working day of each month, semiannual reports, and annual reports, all describing what we were doing and what we had done. Philosophically this made sense. It reinforced accountability, let others know what was going on, and so on. However, realistically, no one read these reports and everyone complained about having to complete them.

So, after futile complaining, I decided to test the system to prove my point. In one of my semiannual reports, I made a mockery of the process and wrote things that, if the report were read, would get me fired.

My secretary, a politically astute and wise professional, advised me to think twice about doing this. But instead we made a bet. I bet her that no one would even notice. I told her to mark her calendar for two weeks later, and if I was right, she owed me five bucks. If she was right, I would pay her out of my severance check. I won the five bucks easily. Not a word was said. Not a ripple was seen.

Feeling a little cocky and self-righteous, I just couldn't let it die now. I went to my boss and "fessed up" in order to lobby for change. He was livid. Instead of being rewarded for uncovering such waste and inefficiency, I was labeled a maverick and a troublemaker. It was rather ironic that this company, which was in a hiring and wage freeze, cutting benefits and downsizing, couldn't accept a cost-saving idea that would also make lots of people happy.

In a company with thousands of employees, this added up to quite an expense. People had to take the time to write these reports every week, month, etc. Someone had to type them, copy them, collate them, route them, file them, and eventually purge and destroy them. Do the math! If you had a "search for QWERTYUIOPS" and rewarded the ideas that saved money, and it was politically correct to uncover such waste and inefficiency, everyone would win. Make it rewarding and culturally correct (see "Get the Point[s]").

Make it fun to poke at the system, and park your egos. We're all in this thing together!

## Whatiffing

Most people know or have been exposed to the concept of brainstorming. This is when you get a group of people together and try to come up with as many ideas as you can about a particular subject or challenge in a very short amount of time. One of the fundamental principles (rules) of the process is to withhold judgment. Remember the three barriers to creativity? Judgmentalism was one of them.

In other words, no matter how silly or unrealistic a person's idea may seem to be, you are instructed to write it down and judge later. Then, the group processes the information, i.e., judges it, combines ideas, etc., with the objective of coming up with something new and worthwhile.

Those of you who have actually participated in one of these brainstorming activities know that judgment is taking place no matter how many rules you have. It's human nature. You also know that the process tends to start quite slowly, in terms of input, because all the participants know that judgment is going on (because they're doing it too!) and remain guarded (self-censoring) in their participation. So, what's the alternative?

Whatiffing takes the brainstorming process one step backward. In other words, before you tackle a real-life problem or issue, the whatiffing process acts as a right-brain lubricant that stimulates weird ideas without the possibility of judgment. For instance, your group will start with a totally unrealistic "what if," such as:

What if everyone could read everyone else's mind?

What if men could have babies?

What if you could make yourself invisible?

What if we went through life in reverse?

What if there was no money in the world?

What if we had eyeballs in our thumbs? (PS: When doing this "what if" at 3M, one group said that instead of wearing contacts, we would start wearing thumbtacks.)

You are supposed to take five to seven minutes to list as many things as you can that would happen if this "what if" were possible—social change, new laws, new products on the market, behaviors, anything that might change as a result of this what if. Then someone reads these lists aloud to the group. What you will see is a rapid ramp-up of activity (unlike traditional brainstorming), high energy, lots of laughter, and difficulty getting people to stop at the end of five to seven minutes. This is not quite the same as brainstorming, first of all because it is fun, but more important, because judgmentalism is impossible. You don't even need the "do not judge" rule, because you cannot judge something that is impossible to begin with. There are no right or wrong, good or bad answers.

So what good is this? As mentioned earlier, it is a ramping-up process. In the next step of the process, rather than jumping right into reality with your real-world issue, you keep a dose of fantasy in the discussion to keep the creative process going and to continue the momentum already developed. For example, let's say we were trying to come up with ways to improve the public education system in the United States. We could sit around and come up with the usual ideas of lengthening the school year, improving student:teacher ratios, better pay and training, etc. These do not take a creative genius to develop (see "Second Right Answers").

Instead, let's take the Department of Education as our reality, and throw a dose of unreality (what if) into the position of the secretary of the Department of Education. For example, "What if Bill Cosby were the secretary of the Department of Education?" How would education change? What would be different in the classroom, the materials, the environment, the curriculum, and so on? What if George Carlin were the secretary of the Department of Education? You can use any name you want for the dose of unreality.

In fact, I was once in a group addressing this exact issue, using the whatiffing process, and our group was assigned Pee Wee Herman as the secretary of education (this was before Pee Wee had his little problem). At the time, my son was at the age when he was watching *Pee Wee's Playhouse* on TV.

Using that as our template, we said that if Pee Wee Herman were secretary of education, classrooms would not have desks bolted to the floor in a row, the furniture would have names, there would be a word for the day, and whenever the students heard that word, they could jump up and down and make a lot of noise, and so forth.

Are these bad ideas? Hardly! If my son had come home from grade school every day with a new word that he had learned and wanted to go back again the next day, I would have considered that progress. You can insert any name you want to into the position you are using, and you can repeat the process with several names to generate even more ideas. But again, judgmentalism is not a problem anymore, because the premise does not allow for it. When you start with an unreal premise, unrealistic ideas are a natural outgrowth, and judgmentalism becomes impossible and nonexistent.

You could adapt this example to organizational change by inserting a variety of unrealistic names into your company's CEO position, or use it for a department by changing who the manager is. It's fun, it works, and people will participate willingly and creatively.

## Let Your Fingers Do the Thinking

Another creative thinking technique involves thought association. Like word association, in which I say a word and you tell me what other words come to mind, this technique draws associations to totally unrelated entities.

Let's say you wanted to look at your business in a totally new light. Take a phone book, open it to the Yellow Pages, and let your fingers do the thinking. Someone starts fanning the pages, and someone else inserts a finger or a pen or a piece of paper at random to select a page. Then someone else takes a stab at the page with eyes closed to select a category. It might be anything from AA (Alcoholics Anonymous or the Automobile Association) to Zoos.

After a category is selected, the group then brainstorms, or what-ifs, how their company or department or whatever other challenge they are working on is like Alcoholics Anonymous. Or, how their company is like a zoo. Who is the ringmaster? How are the animals trained? What makes our zoo better than the others? What liabilities or risks must we assume?

Letting your fingers do the thinking allows people to look at issues, challenges, and solutions from a completely different perspective, with some humor and out-of-the-box thinking. Political correctness is no longer a barrier. Like "whatiffing," this technique also makes weirdness normal.

## Wall of Shame

What is the opposite of a "Wall of Fame"? A "Wall of Shame," of course. But why would any company in its right mind want to showcase its failures? Because fun, innovative companies have a different view of so-called failures. If you knew how many successful products on the market today were the result of past screw-ups, you would start rewarding those who have the guts and initiative to fail more than those who play it safe and never do anything new. ScotchGard, Post-it Notes, and many other products would never have made it to the market had 3M not recognized and rewarded the value of try, try again.

Granted, you need to be a little more selective about the location of a *nontrophy* case, but the objectives are severalfold. For one thing, if you want to develop a culture of creativity, the concept of a "Wall of Shame" creates a safe environment for honest mistakes and reduces the probability that people will hide their less than perfect outcomes.

A second purpose of showcasing past efforts is to tickle the imagination of others in the organization who might be able to piggyback someone else's idea into something of value. After all, one of the objectives of brainstorming is to create great ideas out of a bunch of lousy ones. Why not carry this logic to the point of a visual brainstorming tool, like a "Wall of Shame"?

Finally, a "Wall of Shame" lets us laugh at ourselves, which is another powerful creativity tool. Organizations that take themselves too seriously too much of the time are usually boring, difficult, and stifling places to work. One caveat: I do not recommend posting customer complaint letters in a location that is accessible to current or potential customers. Sharing these may be a great idea for employee training and development, but little can be gained by exposing your warts to the world. Keep the "Wall of Shame" fun and useful as a symbol and a tool of a creative, fun culture.

## Break the Mold

Break the mold is most useful in creating new ways for your customers or your employees (internal customers) to experience your organization. Why would you want to be like everyone else in your industry? As you can read in "Work Smells," because all medical offices smell alike, a simple change like the addition of popcorn, potpourri, or some other positively different smell can have a noticeable effect on the customers' (patients') first and lasting impression.

Carrying that a bit further, "Break the Mold" asks you to look at your organization through the eyes of the customer or employee, depending on the thrust of your effort, and ask yourself, is your business user-friendly? is it pleasurable? is it different, in a good way? If it isn't, then ask how it could be.

There are tons of little things you can do to "wow" people that cost next to nothing. How about dog treats at drive-through windows for customers who come in with Fido? How about greeters in your lobby, instead of a receptionist peeking out over The Great Wall, who can actually show you how to get where you want to go and talk to you along the way (see "Greeters and Minglers"). How about music, entertainment, or games to play while customers are sitting in the lobby waiting for you?

You will notice that all of these examples involve something early in the customer's experience. This is the most important time to show customers that you are different and better. Ideally, you would do this before customers ever come to see you. Maybe on the phone, or in the parking lot. Again, the sky's the limit.

It has been said that people pay for only two things: solutions to problems and good feelings. Which do you sell? If I go to a Disney park, I want to feel good and have fun. If I go to the gas station to fill up my tank, I am solving a problem. I won't have to push my car or walk for miles. Even though I will be spending a fair amount of money in both places, I don't get out of bed in the morning anticipating the experience of filling up my tank, nor do I pull out of a gas station thinking, "Wow, that was fun!"

However, businesses that sell solutions to problems sometimes lose sight of the fact that people's feelings are still there, before, during, and after the sale, and that the only real difference between them and their competition may be how customers "feel" about them. No matter how wonderful a product or service may be, feelings are always involved and always important. After all, gas is gas.

That's where "Break the Mold" comes in. It lets the customer or employee know that this place is different. That the business cares. That it has thought about more than just selling a commodity.

This is particularly important for businesses whose solutions are painful (dentists, lawyers, tax accountants, etc.). My accountant makes house calls. In fact, he goes by the name Dr. Len because he advertises that he does make house calls. He makes the painful process of bookkeeping and paying taxes as pleasant as possible by coming to where you and your records are.

You can and should make people feel better about their experience by "Breaking the Mold" of *normal* expectations.

## How Bad Can It Get?

This is another customer service–oriented brainstorming technique, although it can also be used for other organizational improvements, like your recruitment processes, etc. Rather than looking at the future with the ideal in mind, this technique takes the opposite perspective and asks what the future would look like if we were the absolute worst at whatever we are trying to do. How bad can it get?

For example, if we had the worst customer service, we would not answer our phones, we would put people into voice mail and Touch-Tone hell forever, we would make promises we never intended to keep, we would insult our customers, and so on. Sadly, after this exercise, you may find that you are doing some of the worst possible things to your customers already. It's just that you didn't realize how bad things were until you found that you couldn't imagine much worse. This can be quite an eye-opener for some. The next step is to come up with solutions and then think about "how good can it get?"

For example, one client that did this exercise came up with some very innovative ideas for "how good can it get," things like, "We would anticipate the customers' needs and contact them before they call us." That is, customers would never have to come into the store because we would already know what they wanted and have it delivered.

Even if they sound far-fetched, these ideas are springboards to new services and conveniences, such as shopping online, pick up and delivery, personalized services, and other such innovations.

## Five Whys (aka the Five-Year-Old Consultant)

Those of you who have children know the favorite word of a five-year-old, right? Why? Why? Why? Why? Why? You will notice that there are five whys here. This is a simple, yet effective technique for getting to the root cause of a problem or bottom line of an issue. Like the syndrome that the "Second Right Answer" addresses—i.e., our need to get a lot done quickly—our tendency to stop short in our quest for quick answers also results in our attacking symptoms instead of causes.

Here's a very simple example taken from an automotive technician's diagnosis of a car not starting.

**PROBLEM**

My car wouldn't start this morning.

Why?

Because the ignition wouldn't turn over.

Why?

Because the battery was dead.

**SOLUTION**

Replace or recharge the battery.

In this example, the technician asked why only twice, so he replaced or recharged the battery. A couple of days later, the customer is back with the same complaint.

**PROBLEM**

My car wouldn't start this morning.

Why?

Because the ignition wouldn't turn over.

Why?

Because the battery was dead.

Why?

Because the dome light was on all night.

Why?

Because the door switch didn't turn off.

Why?

Because the door switch was defective.

**SOLUTION**

Replace the door switch.

Can you see where this is going? We could even use more than five whys and ask why the door switch was defective. This might involve solving a problem at the manufacturing level, which might require a whole bunch more whys.

Any time you try to solve a problem or improve a process without attacking the root cause, you are wasting time and money. If you have a morale problem at work, a company picnic isn't going to fix it. *Why* is there poor morale? Because people are demotivated. *Why* are people demotivated? Because they don't think it matters if they work hard. *Why* don't they think it matters? Because no one tells them it does. *Why* doesn't anyone tell them? Because management doesn't think it's important. *Why* doesn't management think it's important? Because managers are evaluated and rewarded for other things.

There is nothing magic about the number five, but the point is to go at least that far before jumping on a solution or a new idea. If you think more whys are needed, keep going. Otherwise, don't waste any more time or money on superficial responses to deeper problems.

## Press Release of the Future

This is a visioning technique that involves projecting what the press might be saying about you or your organization if you are successful in accomplishing your mission, goals, or objectives.

One example of how this technique was used successfully was in educating and exciting an entire workforce about a company's vision and mission statements. A "contest" was set up in which employees were to write a fictitious press release five years into the future with the assumption that the company's vision had been achieved. Not only did this get everyone to learn the vision and mission, but the employees actually applied that learning to a visualized future state. That's the first step to real organizational change.

To ensure thoroughness of thought, be sure that the basic journalistic questions of who, what, when, where, why, and how are answered. In this case, the most important question is the *how*, because this will help define the tangible actions that will need to be taken to realize the company's vision and mission. A follow-on activity is to have a panel of judges made up of a cross section of employees select the best entries in a variety of categories, such as *most creative, most motivating, most competitive,* etc.

Then publish your own newspaper with all the press releases in it and ask for people's reactions, as well as how they plan to put their words into action. This also reduces resistance to change because the future is now desirable, definable, and determined by those who have to make it happen.

## Challenges for Change

As was explained at the beginning of this section, one of the barriers to creative living and thinking is resistance to change. Ironically, most people, when asked, will say that they like change and that they like to try new things. This is a lie, and I can prove it!

As an exercise in minimal, incremental personal change, just try to accomplish one of the following *challenges for change* and stick to it for at least a month, followed by another one the next month, and so on. This may look easy, particularly since you have a month to do each one, but you will probably soon learn that you aren't as adaptable or flexible or open to change as you'd like to think you are.

* Change all the stations on your car radio, and listen to them. No going back.

* Take a different route to or from work and pay attention to what is around you.

* Change something about your daily routine.

* Get lost. Get in your car and go against your instincts to want to know where you are.

* Track down and contact someone from your distant past.

* Change something significant about your appearance. Not just your cologne or your shoes. Pierce something!

* Moonlight. Get a job you like. Do it for something besides money (see "Get a Life").

- Start a new hobby, something out of the ordinary (for you).

- Take a class in something irrelevant (not job-related or work-oriented)

- Read or subscribe to an offbeat publication—something you may disagree with.

- Get to know some weirdoes. Start hanging out with a different crowd for a while.

- Join an organization that wouldn't want you.

The longer-term objective of this effort is to learn to like change, to get more comfortable with it. Every pop psychologist will tell you that change is stressful, as if that were profound. That knowledge alone doesn't change anything. Let's try the "Five Whys" on this one. The second and more important question that needs to be asked is, *why* is change stressful? The answer is that there is a perceived a loss of control. *Why?* Because it's true. You aren't in control. *Why?* Because you didn't have anything to say about it, i.e., you aren't in the driver's seat. *Why?* Because someone else initiated it and you are just expected to adapt.

If you keep going with this root cause analysis, the answer to the problem is that you need to start taking control of change, and the way to do that is to be the initiator of it, not the victim. And, the only way to start to get comfortable with change is on a personal level. That's where the "Challenges for Change" come in.

You will know you are successful with this when you start to enjoy it. In other words, when you start seeing and experiencing the benefits of change, you will actually start seeking out new ways to keep variety and change in your life, and you won't need this list. Ultimately, you will be better at handling and adapting to more significant changes at work and in other aspects of your life, even if someone else initiates them. You will actually become comfortable living outside your old comfort zones.

# Personal Brainspurt Journal

Something that very creative people will tell you is that they get their best ideas at some of the worst possible times and places. In fact, having asked thousands of people when and where they get their "brainspurts" (that's when something pops into your mind spontaneously, as opposed to "brainstorming," when you are actually "trying" to have ideas), fewer than 1 percent say that they get them at work, unless they work at home in their pajamas or in some similarly, positively weird and relaxed environment.

The usual answers are in the car, in the shower, in bed, while gardening, jogging, exercising, and at many other times and places, of which the common denominator is that the person is relaxed, unfocused, and not trying to be creative. Einstein once said that he got his best ideas, not in the laboratory, but in the bathroom while shaving.

Have you ever gone to bed, only to have your mind race and prevent you from sleeping? The problem may be something as simple as, "I have to remember to call Joe tomorrow." You will stay up half the night thinking about this, only to finally fall asleep in the wee hours of the morning and wake up to the alarm trying to remember what it was that kept you up half the night. That's a lose-lose. You lost sleep, and you even lost the idea that caused you to lose sleep. Don't count sheep. Don't meditate. Don't get up and have a drink of anything. Just *write it down!*

You don't have to get out of bed, turn on the light, go to a desk, and write legibly between the lines. Have a blank piece of paper and pencil or pen ready to go on the nightstand so that you can just roll over, jot down "call Joe," and go back to sleep. Now you have saved both the thought and your sleep. That's a win-win. Some people use a pocket recorder. Others use index cards. Whatever works best for you is fine, but save the thought.

In fact, I used to call this the "cocktail napkin" technique because after a presentation or day of training, I might unwind in the hotel lounge and decompress. Without fail, I would start to have brainspurts about what I could have done better, what I could add to a certain section, etc., and because I did not have paper and pen handy, I would habitually just grab a cocktail napkin and jot down the key words so that I would remember the thought later. At the end of the week, when I unpacked my bags, I would have this wad of cocktail napkins, which I then filed in a folder called "Cocktail Napkins." Then, when I had the time to revisit and revise that particular program, I would merely pull out the napkins and *voilá!* My work was done.

On a little deeper level, understand that we each have our own personal cycles that cause us to have these brainspurts at certain times more than at others. Start keeping your "Personal Brainspurt Journal" with you at all times, and every time you get an idea, write it down, *and* write down where and when you got it. After about a month of doing this, you will start to notice a pattern. This technique will help you get a fix on when you are most likely to be creative and to have ideas, i.e., your personal cycles and situations.

Eventually, you can even program your brain to think about specific challenges. At the top of a page in your journal, write down the question you are trying to solve or the challenge you are working to overcome and plant that seed in your brain for the future. You may not get answers to all your problems, and the answers you do get may not develop right away, but every idea generated in this manner is a freebie. You didn't have to work to get it. In fact, some of the best ideas in this book were written horizontally at three o'clock in the morning.

People who use and understand this process rave about its success. I know of an advertising executive who gets her best ideas while in the shower before going to work in the morning. Being creative is her livelihood, so getting freebies in the shower is a blessing. To capitalize upon her creative cycle, she installed a whiteboard with markers in her shower, so that she can write down her ideas as they come to her. She then transfers them to her daily planner, goes to work, and develops them. Half of her daily mental work is done before she leaves the house. And as we all know by now, the odds are against her having the same quantity or quality of ideas while in the office. There are just too many distractions, interruptions, and other demands for your attention to let you be creative at work.

Abraham Lincoln may have said it best: ". . . often an idea would occur to me which seemed to have FORCE. . . . I never let one of those ideas escape me, but wrote it on a scrap of paper and put it in that drawer. In that way I saved my best thoughts on the subject, and, you know, such things often come in a kind of intuitive way more clearly than if one were to sit down and deliberately reason them out." To save the results of such mental action is true intellectual economy. As a bonus, the more we honor the muse, the more it shows up, and the more moments of inspiration we can count on having.

Now, get your journal and start recording your brainspurts as they come to you. Write down any ideas that pop into your head, whether they are completely original and unrelated to anything you are reading, or just enhancements of existing ideas in the book. Just do it! You will want to remember these ideas anyway, but when you get to the end of the book, there will be a reward in it for you—although the personal reward of creative thinking and problem solving should be enough.

# WEIRD IDEAS TO WIN ToDAY'S TALENT

## aka RECRUITMENT

*Finding, attracting, and hiring the best and the brightest people is one of the top challenges facing most organizations today. The scarcest commodity in business is not customers or technology or ideas or capital. It's talent. And, difficulty in recruitment is not just a function of supply and demand or low unemployment rates. It is not just a function of money, either. Those are easy scapegoats for a lack of creativity in recruitment practices. You have no control over those things, so it's easy to hang your blame hat on things that you can't do anything about.*

*Let's talk about things you can control. Ironically, these are the same things that really matter to the people you want to hire. Things like, What's it like to work here? What kind of people succeed here? What do people do for fun around here? Is there any fun at all? Is this place a bureaucracy, or can you really get things done around here? Will my boss be a jerk? These are the things people want to know.*

*This section covers where to find people, what to tell them, how to wow them, and even how to get them back if they do leave.*

# #1 All the Right Places

Anyone in public relations or advertising will tell you that favorable press coverage or published articles are better than paid-for advertising any day, and they're free! So why not find ways, whenever and wherever possible, to get your company and your people in the press in a positive light? A press release announcing a new hire, a promotion, an award, or any other good news not only is good PR for your company, but is also a powerful and free way to recognize and reward your people.

The second important piece of this idea is to be sure to send these press releases to the publications that are important to your employees, as well as to you. In other words, send your notices of new hires, promotions, awards, etc., to *their* hometown newspapers, *their* professional journals, *their* associations, *their* clubs, *their* college press, and any other places where they will be seen and recognized in their own circles of influence, past and present.

Another benefit of this idea is the positive exposure your company will get in common recruiting circles, especially in the college papers and professional journals. People notice people with whom they have places and backgrounds in common, and they especially notice if their comrades are experiencing success or recognition. If you found one great employee from this school, town, or association, there's a decent chance that there might be another one there.

The easiest and best way to make this idea work is to have a press photo for every employee and new hire and have them fill out a publicity form with the name, address, and any other contact information for any publications, organizations, etc., that they would like to have notified in the event a press release is sent out. This not only makes it easier for you to keep up to date, but can also serve as a consent form by the employee as well. It's free, it's easy, and it works.

# #2 All the Wrong Places

Do you advertise for employees in the "Help Wanted" section of the paper? If so, you are probably listing your ad in the right category, right? Wrong! This idea is twofold. First, it means advertising for your traditional types of candidates (i.e., those who already have the title and the experience) in nontraditional places. Second, it means looking for nontraditional candidates (i.e., those who never had the title, but have relevant, transferable experience).

For example, let's say you want a customer service representative. If you run your ad in the sales and customer service section, you have already limited your options and your market. You are looking in the same box that everyone else is. And, your targets are now looking at your competitors' ads right next to yours. That's a lose-lose!

You are also targeting the active job seeker, rather than the passive candidate who may be more valuable to you. Top talent is usually already gainfully employed and does not need to read the help wanted ads. If your company sells sporting equipment, try advertising your opportunities in the sports section. Not only do your type of people read that section every day, but there is also little or no competition for your ad. You stand out, and you also have a better chance of being seen by both active and passive job seekers.

Think about the demographics of your ideal candidates and put your advertising in places where they will see it, not just in the classifieds. This same theory applies to other types of publications, journals, programs, and specialized print media, as well as newspapers. Using the same example, if your company sells sporting goods, you could advertise in sporting publications or at sporting events.

Now let's look at the second wrong place. Who else might have valuable experience and training in customer service environments, but may not have had the title? Maybe a waitress, or a bartender, or a flight attendant, or a teacher. Look for people with skills rather than just people with titles. "All the Wrong Places" involves getting out of the traditional "been there, done that" category boxes and looking at transferable skills and trainability. There are tons of frustrated workers looking to do something new with the skills they have already developed. But unless you, as employer, open that door, most people will either rule themselves out or not even realize they could have been candidates in the first place.

Rather than hope that people figure this out, start advertising and promoting your job opportunities in "All the Wrong Places." Advertise in trade and interest publications and be totally aboveboard about it. Say, "Are you a frustrated waitress?" or "Are you tired of teaching?" and then explain how such a person might start over with you.

This idea can go beyond advertising. Go to trade fairs, job fairs, and other visibility functions that attract your cross-market. In fact, the venue doesn't have to have anything to do with recruiting. Cisco Systems actually gave away tickets in the end zones at Stanford games in exchange for having the people stand up with a series of placards that spelled out www.cisco.com/ careers. The idea was to promote Cisco's recruiting Web site during touchdowns and extra point attempts. What better place than in a captive bowl full of candidates?

Cisco also had a booth at the Flower and Garden Show in the San Francisco Bay Area. The company's logic was that people who could afford to have enough property to have gardens in the Bay Area were probably successful people. And, in the San Francisco Bay Area, that group has to include a pretty large number of techies. Cisco went to them in a unique environment (theirs), and demonstrated that it knew who they were. One of the best things about this concept is that there is little or no competition; you get exclusive exposure, and ultimately you get the pick of the litter.

United Parcel Service (UPS) set up job booths at a Metallica concert (a heavy-metal rock band), with the objective of driving candidates to its Web site. Motorola, IBM, and AT&T have sponsored "Spring Break" (the annual mass migration to Florida by students looking for a wild and crazy escape between semesters), generating hundreds of applications.

In fact, you don't have to limit this to advertising. Don't you have a favorite waiter or waitress? Haven't you seen exemplary customer service in action when you had a problem as a consumer? Look at sales clerks, cashiers, pizza delivery guys/gals, hotel employees, the concierge, valets, amusement park workers, theater employees, auto salespeople, car washers, dry cleaners, home repair and maintenance workers, maids and pet sitters, telephone customer service/help desk workers, and on and on and on. (Also see "WYSIWYG.") You and every one of your employees is exposed to top-notch talent almost every day, but you never think about looking at them as potential recruits, because they are in "All the Wrong Places!"

Now, let's take this idea to the extreme. Would you like a really captive market? One that has its own work space already? One that isn't going anywhere for a long time? One that has no choice but to show up for work? If so, then think about hiring convicts to work as telecommuters from prison. Now, hold on! Think about it.

There are plenty of "programs" out there designed to get ex-felons and other lawbreakers back to work after being released. In some ways, that's riskier than hiring them while they are still imprisoned. They can't steal office supplies while they are in prison. They are no risk to fellow employees while they are in prison. And, you can be assured that if they are supposed to be working certain hours and you have an agreement with the warden and the staff, then they will be working as scheduled, while they are in prison!

This arrangement can be used for more than just menial labor, like stuffing envelopes or routine phone work. Many convicts are both willing and able to learn and perform high-level assignments. If they can teach themselves law and get other degrees on their own, without any other incentive, then they can just as easily learn to become software developers, beta testers, system architects, or almost anything else, if given the opportunity, the tools, and the training.

In addition to developing a new source of "captive" labor, you can also be a hero in the community for contributing to the rehabilitation of some of society's down and out. Then, if and when they are released, they have a track record and are immediately employable for meaningful work. Now, that's an incentive!

If employers today are willing to rob the cradle and hire kids just out of high school, without their degrees, and train them, then this should be a no-brainer. Start looking and advertising in "All the Wrong Places" and your recruiting sources and successes will multiply overnight (also see "Are You Talking to Me?").

## #3 WYSIWYG

Computer geeks and freaks know that this is an acronym for "what you see is what you get," meaning that what you see on the computer screen is what you will get when you print it out. In recruitment, I use this term to encourage you to look at the people working in or for your organization who are not directly employed by you, i.e., outside contractors, temps, building service workers, delivery people, couriers, and so on. Which ones are always there, always on time, always working hard, have a pleasant personality, and so forth? What you see is what you get! Offer them a job working for you.

Similar in concept to "All the Wrong Places," this idea allows you to actually see the person in action. Although temporary service firms frown upon having their best people stolen, unless you have a contract that strictly prohibits it (usually it is allowed in exchange for a fee), the days of indentured servitude are over. No one owns these workers. Go get 'em!

They could be contract consultants working on a special project. They could be maintenance workers who are hired by your building/landlord. They could be window washers. They could be repairmen (or women) from one of the utility companies. They could be delivery people (everything from express packages to pizza). They could work for cleaning services. The bottom line is, look at every single person in or around your building and watch her or him work. If you like what you see, then you'll also like what you get. WYSIWYG!

# #4 What's Your Sign?

There is a recruiting philosophy pioneered by Southwest Airlines that embraces the concept "hire for attitude—train for skill." This same approach has been adopted by many other organizations that place great value on maintaining their culture. Skills have less impact on culture, fit, and customer service than one's attitudes toward work and life in general.

So, how do you go about identifying someone's "attitude"? Aside from the variety of personality and psychological instruments on the market, you can just ask the right questions. Don't get bogged down in asking things that are already on the résumé or that you can find out elsewhere (like in a background check).

Here are a dozen examples of the types of weird questions you might want to start asking:

* What's your personal motto?

* Tell me your favorite joke.

* You've got one seat left in your fallout shelter. Who gets it?

* If you could have dinner with anyone, living or dead, who would it be, and why?

* Have you ever broken the rules? Why? What was the outcome?

* What's the first thing you usually do at work in the morning?

* Did you ever use your sense of humor to get out of a jam? When and how?

* Describe yourself in three words.

* Tell me about one of your most embarrassing moments.

* What's the most important thing your parents taught you?

* What do you want to be when you grow up?

- Tell me about the worst boss you ever had, and how you handled him or her.

The point here is that there is no one right answer to any of these questions. They are ways to get insight into someone's thought processes, ability to handle ambiguity, sense of humor, candor, humility, and a whole host of other insights that do not come out of traditional interview questions.

To quote Yahoo!, the Internet search firm in Santa Clara, California, "We want people who are passionate about their subject areas. And it turns out that most people who have a passion for something specific like sports, arts, culture, also have a passion for life. It's not just about doing great things for the company, but also great things in life."

In fact, just as a side note, an easy way to shift your interviewing paradigm is not to call it an interview. Think of it as a conversation. If you were meeting someone new in a social setting, wouldn't your questions be more interesting than those in a typical job interview? The whole point is to get to know the person. Now, come up with your own list of "weird" questions that reveal the real person inside, without breaking the law.

# #5 Postnuptials

Most employers who conduct exit interviews do them during the person's last days or even *on* his or her last day of employment. Although this is better than not doing an exit interview at all, it doesn't really serve your purposes as well as it could. Instead of an instant exit interview (which is for you, *not* for the departing employee), send flowers or some other gift to the person's home (not to the new employer!) congratulating the person and wishing him or her well in the new job. Now, that makes a statement.

Then, wait a couple of weeks after the person has started the new job and then send your exit questionnaire. Better yet, set up a phone interview; best of all, arrange to meet the person over coffee (or, for techies, M&M's, Coke, or beer) to discuss it. Not only will the person be more candid, but he or she will have a better sense of how the new job and employer compare with working for you. Just as in "What's Your Sign?" try to approach this more as a conversation than as an interview.

This is your opportunity to start planting some seeds for the person's return (aka boomerang strategies), particularly if the honeymoon is over and the period of blissful ignorance has started to wane. Other ideas that can give you ways to plant those seeds are "Bridge Over Troubled Waters," "'Get Out of Jail Free' Card," "Missing You," and "Opportunity Knocks."

## #6 "Get Out of Jail Free" Card

I am amazed that in this day and age of talent demand and shortages, there are still employers out there who would never consider "letting" someone who had left "the company" come back. Whom are you punishing? If that same person applied for a job with your company, but had *not* worked for you before, would you hire him or her? If so, that means it is better to *not* have a track record with your company.

Face it, if you hire the best and the brightest, it stands to reason that those people will be the hardest to hold onto. Anyone can hold onto a loser. If you have very low turnover, before you break your arm patting yourself on the back, be sure that it isn't because you have people no one else wants.

If you know for a fact that you would hire a particular ex-employee (for example, if she has a rare talent, you know it, and you'll always need it), give her a "get out of jail free" card that entitles her to immediate reemployment without having to go through Human Resources or any other bureaucratic process requirements.

"You want a job? You got it!" This is a powerful symbolic gesture that reinforces an employee's value to you and leaves him or her with a very positive last (and lasting) impression of what he or she is leaving. He or she can escape the jail of your competition at any time.

Human Resources people often bristle at such an idea, and are quick to ask, "What about references and background checks, and all the other preliminary work that has to be done?" Why do you need to check references or complete any other preemployment requirements for such people? You already hired them once, and they have obviously proven themselves or you wouldn't want them back, right? You've already got something better than references or credentials; you've got past performance!

If it is really necessary, make the hiring offer contingent upon whatever security blankets you need, but you surely don't need to go back before the date you hired such a person before! Not only is that a waste of time and money, but it sure doesn't say much for your process the first time around. Just be sure to make it clear on the "Get Out of Jail Free Card" that the offer is contingent upon a suitable position being available and that current employees have first priority.

There are other benefits to rehiring former employees as well. They can come in running, they know the culture and they fit into it, they do not need an orientation to your policies or procedures, they know the people and the processes, *and* they have fresh ideas and perspectives from having been outside your box for a while. Need I go on?

## #7 Bridge Over Troubled Waters

When a high performer leaves, don't let your ego get in the way of your success as an employer. Show regret, wish the person well, and tell the person that you would love to have him or her back if the new employment situation doesn't work out the way he or she hopes it will.

Next, to capitalize on the fact that the honeymoon period always ends, tell these high performers that if they return to your company within one year, you will not only restore their prior service, but also "bridge" their service for the time they were gone (i.e., they will be treated as if they had never left). This means that their vacation schedule is reinstated and any other perks of tenure continue to build as if they had never left you. Datatel (a software solutions company based in Fairfax, Virginia) is a perfect case in point. It warmly refers to its rehires as "retreads" and gives full credit for prior service toward what it calls "time-based benefits" *regardless* of how long ago they terminated.

Think about this. It costs nothing if these people do not exercise the option, and next to nothing if they do, but it plants a seed in their brains that for the next year they can defect from your competition and be kept whole by coming back to you. They can have their cake and eat it too. If you have to justify it another way, think of such people as having been on a leave of absence or a sabbatical. The ROI (return on investment) on this incentive is huge if you recover valuable talent. The bottom line is, employees who leave and come back are the most loyal employees you will ever have.

There are several other twists that you can put on this incentive. For example, what if the first year passes and you still want to lure someone back? Offer to restore but not bridge the person's service. Or, you can add the caveat that this bridge or restoration of service will not take effect until the person has been back with you for at least another year. Don't just reward returning, reward retention as well.

You can design the parameters any way you want. Just be sure you apply the criteria consistently and legally.

Again, this is a very inexpensive yet effective way of keeping your hooks in former employees for as long as possible, to start realizing a return on your prior investment, to steal them back from the competition, and to maximize retention all at the same time.

## #8 Missing You

Just as your college uses alumni associations to keep in touch and keep you contributing, your company can do the same. It's not a sign of failure to have a lot of ex-employees. It may even be a sign of success: Your graduates are in demand! The only problem is that you paid for their tuition. Do you want to recoup your investment?

Create a database of alumni and keep in touch, both electronically and by hard copy. Invite them to appropriate company events (announcements, annual meetings, socials, etc.). Send them your newsletter, press releases, and other positive communications so that they not only remember you exist, but see that you are doing well, even without them. Again, treat them as if they were on leave or sabbatical. They're not dead!

Booz-Allen & Hamilton really put some muscle behind their alumni efforts. They actually created a position called manager of alumni programs and made that person responsible for managing the database (over 3,000 alumni) and coordinating the publishing of an alumni directory. The directory, which goes to all alumni, lists names alphabetically, the year the alumnus or alumna left the firm, and cross-references for geography and even former surnames. Bain & Co., a Boston-based international consulting firm, have more people in their alumni association than they have on their payroll!

Even better, personalize this process. Assign your alumni to various "linkages" (i.e., current employees) within the company who will manage the relationship and keep in touch in other ways. They can attach personal notes to your alumni mailings, or even call them or meet with them on occasion. You can even create an incentive for the linkage people in the event one of their alums returns to the fold (see "Bird Dog Biscuits").

A trickle-down benefit to maintaining good relationships with former employees is that they will continue to speak well of you. In Focus Systems, Inc., a manufacturer of computer projectors based in Wilsonville, Oregon, is a good case in point. As a result of its alumni program, it gets referrals from former employees all the time. People will call and say that they just interviewed so and so, and he or she was really good, but they did not have the right position for him or her, so they are referring the person to you.

One last suggestion: Be sure to get an e-mail address for people when they leave, and preferably not their work address, but rather their personal e-mail address at home. This is a very effective way to stay in touch with large numbers of people after they leave. It's quick and nonintrusive.

Leaving your company should not be viewed as a betrayal. It is natural for valuable talent to pursue new opportunities. Remember, your best people are the ones who are most likely to leave, because they are the best people. Get them back! I recall one client, a CPA firm, that even rehired an average employee so that others in the firm could see that the grass isn't always greener on the other side of the fence.

## #9 Opportunity Knocks

If you have an internal job posting process, why not put your alumni (i.e., ex-employees) on the distribution list? The placement office is just another benefit of having graduated from your company. To avoid offending your current employees, alumni can go into a second-tier priority status.

In other words, for positions that are not filled by current employees, your alumni get preference over the rest of the world. Not only does that dangle another carrot in front of a potentially disenchanted alum, but it is also a whole lot cheaper and more reliable than using headhunters or traditional advertising. And as was mentioned in "Missing You," they may even refer someone else to your company.

Forrester Research, Inc., of Cambridge, Massachusetts, is a good example of this concept. In fact, Forrester built a Web site and common network where they post jobs and offer a referral bonus to former employees who refer candidates that get hired (also see "Bird Dog Biscuits"). Forrester anticipates that some of the former employees will be attracted to the current jobs and will throw their own hats into the ring.

And don't forget, as it says in "Monica" (Idea 19), put your interns on the list too.

# #10 Homecoming Celebration

So, let's say one of these boomerang strategies works. Your alumnus has come back! This is cause for celebration, so take advantage of the opportunity to showcase your success. If you're a technology or other high-performance company, you probably already know how to have fun. Rehiring a former employee is a great excuse for showing off, both internally and externally.

Send out publicity and press releases to both your local media and the media in the alum's hometown, college press, etc. (see "All the Right Places"). After all, that's where you found this person. What a great testimonial to you as an employer—people who leave actually come back. And don't forget to send a copy of the homecoming invitation to your boomerangs-to-be. Get them thinking, too!

Have a party. Get a decorated cake, confetti, the whole thing. After all, look at all the money you saved by not paying headhunters or advertisers, and not hiring an unknown. Oh, and by the way, be sure one of the gifts is an engraved boomerang.

# #11 Birds of a Feather

Finding and recruiting the best and the brightest talent has become as much an art as a science. That's why you have to do more than just sell yourself and your company. This is especially true with entry-level and younger candidates, who place great emphasis on the quality of their nonwork life, their peers, and other so-called intangibles.

"Birds of a Feather" is a way to involve non-Human Resources, peer-level people in the recruitment process. They can serve as hosts, tour guides, or in any other role that allows your candidate to get to know firsthand someone who has already been through what she or he is considering. Because they are of the same general age, background, and experience, there is also an enhanced credibility and connection.

Cisco Systems starts the connection on their Web site. The "Make Friends @ Cisco" icon begins a process of establishing an e-mail pen pal. The objective is to connect potential recruits to real people in the company. What's in it for Cisco employees? A referral bonus (see "Bird Dog Biscuits") if the person is eventually hired! The referring employees also get a Cisco Lotto Card. Lotto winners receive mugs, athletic bags or some other logo paraphernalia.

And, to demonstrate to prospects that Cisco has a practical sense of humor, there is even a button on the Web site that says "Oh, no! My boss is coming," which when clicked immediately pulls up a new screen with the "Seven Habits of Highly Successful Employees" or "Gifts for Bosses & Co-workers." After all, most people surf for new jobs while at work in their current one, regardless of policies intended to restrict such behavior.

Let's take it a step further. If and when an out-of-town candidate is invited to visit your company, the peer host can pick her up at the airport, show her around the area, escort her through the interview day and generally be an "at-ease link" in the recruitment process.

This idea not only is a real plus for the candidate, but can also be positioned as a perk for the host employee. Many employees would love to get away from the daily grind once in a while to represent the company in this way. This is particularly true of people who are in jobs that do not have a lot of outside activities or contact.

One caveat, however: Any non-Human Resources people you involve in the recruitment process should be trained. Perhaps a group orientation for peer hosts could cover the dos and don'ts of recruitment (i.e., the types of questions and inquiries that are off limits and why), what their role is and isn't, what routes to take to and from the airport to give the best impression, what to do in the event of a problem, and so on.

Even though the host may not be conducting interviews and you may not consider him to be part of the selection process, the law may see things differently, since valuable insights may be obtained during the candidates' nonstructured times with their peer hosts. At the end of the visit, allow your peer hosts to complete a simple observation form, which is completely optional and open-ended.

You've got nothing to lose and everything to gain. Just be aware that your host can now be legally construed to be a participant in the screening process, which is why some basic training in recruitment (dos and don'ts) is essential.

## #12 Hire Times

OK, so you've scheduled a complete day of interviews, tours, and other hoops for your candidate to jump through. Where's the fun? A great deal of this book is devoted to ways of making your workplace more fun and letting the world know about it. If all of the variables by which a recruit measures you (pay, benefits, work duties, etc.) are fairly similar to your competition, how do you differentiate yourself so that more people want to work for you than for them (see "Gimme Three Words")?

If you plan to use the "Birds of a Feather" idea, why not carry it a step further and invite other peer-level employees and their partners to join the candidate for some local fun and entertainment? This not only shows that your company and people know how to have fun, but also fills your candidate's need to see what the local area has to offer beyond a job.

Research has shown that most candidates' top concern, after "What's it like to work here?" is "What's it going to be like to live here, for me and my family?" Therefore, to really do this thing right, be sure to invite the candidate's partner to join him or her for the visit as well. After all, this will usually be a joint decision, so why not demonstrate that you understand, appreciate, and support this consideration?

If cost is an issue, wait until the second visit, if there needs to be one. However, I would suggest streamlining your process so that you can get it all done in one visit. Not only will you save more than enough money to afford to invite the candidate's partner, but you will also be communicating that you are an action-oriented company.

One company that does it all is Trilogy. When Trilogy flies its top candidates into town, along with girlfriends, boyfriends, spouses, or partners, for a three-day visit, a dozen or more "Trilogians" join them on Sixth Avenue, the hub of Austin, Texas, nightlife. A morning of grueling, highly technical interviews might be followed by an afternoon of mountain biking, in-line skating, or laser tag. Even if you make a great first impression, the last impression can be just as important.

As a footnote, be sure to let your candidates know, *in advance*, that these options will be available to them *and* their guests so that they not only have a positive anticipation, but also can pack and plan accordingly. And have the peer host(s) ask the candidates and their partners, *in advance*, what types of activities they prefer so that proper arrangements can be made for a successful visit.

## #13 Wanna Trade?

When human resources personnel at ServiceWare walk through the halls where they produce customer care software, they typically hear the staff oohing and aahing about the hottest new science fiction films. Thus, when a marketing company approached ServiceWare about a recruiting thrust tied to a popular sci-fi flick, the light bulb clicked on. The result was perhaps one of the most unusual one-time recruiting events: a special showing of George Lucas's *Star Wars: Episode 1, The Phantom Menace* at two theaters located in what ServiceWare defined as "candidate-rich" locales.

About six weeks before the scheduled commercial debut of the film, ServiceWare placed a large ad in the local papers' Sunday classified section featuring a galactic theme and artwork and offering two free tickets for submission of a quality résumé. The company also produced a series of introductory slides promoting the company. (Lucas would not permit full-motion video to immediately precede the showing.)

What is the learning point? Find ways to trade (barter) something your recruits want in exchange for something you want (résumés). You can combine this with the "Rock Me, Baby!" idea and offer tickets to a concert. Or tweak the "All the Wrong Places" idea and give away tickets to sporting events. Set up a booth outside the event several hours or a half-day in advance and be very specific about what types of candidates and résumés will qualify for the tickets. Make it a tailgate party.

Identify your primary market of candidates and what activities and "things" they like, then offer a barter. Keep up with concerts and other special events coming to your area and buy tickets in bulk. Or, if you really want to make a splash, sponsor the event. Then get the word out. Believe me, if you build it, they will come. The best way to find out what types of barters would have the most appeal is to ask the people you already have, who are of the same ilk. Maybe those with the best ideas can serve as hosts.

As is the case with most of the ideas in this book, your options are almost unlimited. Just find out what would have the greatest appeal (and don't forget to leverage the public relations impact), then go for it!

# #14 Bozo Filters

We've talked a lot about how to get people to *want* to work for you, but we haven't talked about how to get candidates who don't have the right stuff to leave you alone, i.e., to screen themselves out.

The technical term for this is a realistic job preview, or RJP. Perhaps the worst example of an RJP is the old Army recruiting commercial, which said, "It's not a job; it's an adventure!" The commercial showed people traveling the world, skydiving, riding in tanks, and doing all sorts of exciting things.

Let's assume that you had no idea what the true Army experience might be like, and you relied solely on this portrayal of it. You take the Army up on the deal, and the next thing you know, they shave your head, kick your butt, and remove any sense of identity you may have brought with you. That's not a realistic job preview. Can you see any similarities to your company's recruiting message?

Unfortunately, in the Army you can't just quit. But in the free world of work, you can. And selling people a bill of goods only to have them find out later that they made a big mistake is a lose-lose. The employee loses, and the employer loses.

So, more intelligent organizations are creating valid ways to give potential recruits the good, the bad, and the ugly so that their decision making is based on reality, which ultimately reduces turnover and other morale-related problems. Granted, your offer/acceptance ratio goes down, meaning that it takes more candidates in the queue to get to the other side, but it costs a whole lot more in time and money to hire a bunch of misfits, resulting in low morale and high turnover and the need to start all over again.

The term *bozo filter* was coined by Alan Cooper of the former Cooper Software in reference to a preinterview test on his company Web site. He says, "I don't talk to bozos anymore because 90 percent of them turn away when they see our test. It is a self-administering bozo filter."

One question asked prospective software engineers to design a new table-creation feature for Microsoft Word. They were asked to provide pencil sketches and a description of the new user interface. Another question, for design communicators, asked them to develop a marketing strategy for a new Touch-Tone phone aimed at consumers from the year 1850. Candidates submitted their entries, and Cooper routed them around the company for feedback. Only the candidates with the highest marks got interviews.

Good candidates actually love this, which is the whole point. One design communicator said the test told him more about the real job than any job description could. A software designer said, "It was a fun puzzle, much more engaging than most of what I was doing on my prior job."

Interestingly, Cooper said that he gets e-mail from some people asking, "Before I take this test, is the position still open?" He says no because he doesn't want anyone who sees it as a chore. If they don't like the test, they won't like the job.

Inacom created the "World Tour Game," which is an on-line test disguised as a game. There are three levels, and if you make it to the third level, you get a job offer and are entered into a raffle for a $1,500 prize. Ernst & Young's Web site has "Strategy Zone," which has interactive case studies with actual types of client situations. Visitors to the Web site submit their analysis and recommendations, and Ernst & Young grades them and sends them back. The target market is high-potential MBAs.

Even if you don't go to these extents, you can still improve your bozo filters by writing more honest and candid ads that mention long hours, difficult customer contact, or whatever else may be a rude awakening after you put people on the payroll. Continue to promote the positives of working for your company, but also save yourself and your candidates a lot of agony by allowing and encouraging people to screen themselves out now, instead of having them quit or be fired later.

This holds true for the interview process as well. It should be more than a sales pitch. Ask people how they feel about occasional long hours, travel, or whatever the potential downsides may be. You'll be doing both of you a favor.

## #15 Headhunter Hostage Pay

OK, so maybe you can't rely exclusively on your in-house recruiters—which means that it may be time to go to the "out-house" recruiters. But who says you can't change the way they are paid? They work for you, don't they? With the trend toward pay for performance on the rise, start looking at how you pay *everyone*, including your third-party service providers. This idea can be applied to more than just headhunters.

Pay drives behavior. If you pay headhunters for finding people, that's what they'll do. Whenever I speak to a room full of recruiters, employment managers, and the like, and suggest paying for retention or success, they look at me like I have two heads. (I think that's the reason.) That's not the way it's done! Says who?

There are plenty of search firms that will guarantee their placements for thirty to ninety days, which usually means that they will offer you a credit toward the next search, as if it's OK to keep trying and failing. You've lost a lot more than the cost of the fee already! But few, if any, will offer to tie any portion of their fee to the person's actually staying and doing the job. Even used cars have warranties!

Here's an offer they can't refuse: Offer to pay *more* than normal. Now you've got their attention. If the person stays for a certain period of time (maybe a year) *and* if key, clearly defined performance objectives are met, the search firm will be eligible for a performance bonus or some other incentive, like first preference in future searches. You can create whatever incentive you want, but if it is above and beyond the "normal" compensation, the search firm has no room to complain. My suggestion is to make the base fee less than standard, with a kicker (the added incentive) that can take it above the standard fee.

The first response you will get from headhunters is that they have no control over these things. However, headhunters do have control over sending you people with the core competencies and credentials, if you, the employer, can identify them. In fact, it's their responsibility to do so. Headhunters are paid to screen and select, not just to find warm bodies. And, if they are not willing to get paid more than usual for doing more than usual, find another firm.

You can apply this pay for performance concept to any number of variables, but the biggest ones should be retention and performance. And you should be willing and able to pay a premium (albeit a minimal one) for someone who stays long enough and contributes significantly enough to provide a return on your investment. Another way to tie the longer-term value to the headhunter's compensation is to tie the headhunter's bonus to the employee's first-year pay, rather than to the hiring salary. This works only if you have a strong pay for performance plan in place already. And if you do, the better the person performs, the more the headhunter stands to earn, too.

The managing director for the Chicago-based recruiting firm A. T. Kearney actually recommends this type of gain sharing for his firm. For example, in one case, the firm negotiated with a *Fortune 100* technology company to place executives in a new, high-end sales operation. In exchange, the firm earns bonuses based on the sales performance of the executives they place.

Some companies are actually paying outside consultants in equity (stock). The Parthenon Group, a Boston management consulting firm, is one that accepts equity payments. They give up a portion of a generous fee to build an investment portfolio that includes a hot new company. The advantage to the client is that it encourages consultants to focus on long-term success, rather than quick fixes. It also increases the odds that the consultants will perform at their best because they stand to profit from your profit. It ties both client and vendor to the same goal(s). It's now a shared risk, instead of a one-sided deal.

Smaller companies and start-ups are particularly suited for this type of arrangement because they usually have limited cash, but also have lots of potential (they hope). It also allows smaller or younger companies to start utilizing the services of outside consultants and benefiting from their expertise earlier than they might otherwise be able to afford under traditional fee-for-services arrangements. Hold 'em hostage for their bounty!

# #16  Secondhand References

Let's face it, no one in her or his right mind would ever give you the name of someone as a reference if that person wasn't going to say great things about her or him. That's why references are seldom called, and if they are, they are seldom (almost never) negative. So what's the point?

The next time someone gives you the name of a personal reference, call. But, after you have heard all the wonderful things the reference has to say about the person, thank her or him and then, in a rather casual, off-the-cuff way, say, "Oh, by the way (that's called the Columbo technique), do you know anyone else who might know this person?" Of course the reference does! Don't say, "Could you give me some more references?" When you ask the person if he or she knows anyone else who knows this person, there is little chance that the person can say no.

And don't ask for names of friends. You don't need to talk to friends. If you did, you could just stick to the references you already have. You want to talk to people whom your candidate did not expect you to talk to, like former bosses, coworkers, suppliers, vendors, customers, etc. This is perfectly legal and perfectly acceptable if you have a signed disclosure as part of your application process. That's the section at the very end with all the fine print that says that by signing this application the candidate consents to any form of background investigation, credit report, criminal history, etc.

# #17 DORK

As with "Postnuptials," the concept of delaying your offer rejection questionnaire makes sense, too. The traditional reason for surveying people who do not accept your offers of employment is to find out where you came up short, whether you could have had any control over it, and how to improve your odds in the future.

In "DORK" (Delayed Offer Rejection Kwestionnaire), the idea is to wait a little while before going back to the well. Ideally, try to set up a face-to-face meeting, maybe over coffee or a beer. Give it a few weeks at least, and maybe even a couple of months. You might even consider using the person's peer host in the process (see "Birds of a Feather").

By doing so, you are adding another potential benefit to the process. Buyer's remorse may have set in. The honeymoon is over, and the reality of the new position and employer may not be all it was cracked up to be. (Also see "Postnuptials.")

Some will say that you need to get an immediate response so that the information is fresh in the candidate's mind. If you are stuck in that paradigm, go ahead and give the candidate a brief, traditional questionnaire if you wish. But hold open the option of having a more "real" discussion later. The candidate's impression of you may be freshest right after the offer, but you lose the opportunity for him or her to have a basis for comparing it to the offer that he or she actually accepted.

"DORK" does not assume failure, but rather another chance to win. It's intended not just to get information, but to influence, too.

## #18 Lucy in the Sky With Diamonds

No, this is not a reference to drugging your people. It is an example of one of many creative ways to get your message, whatever it is, in front of the right people in weird places and in weird ways that will be noticed and remembered.

"Lucy in the Sky With Diamonds" refers to using airplanes to fly over crowds with sky banners or even using skywriting. This was done at Apple Computer headquarters a number of years ago on the day of Apple's annual meeting, at which the company was announcing less than stellar financial results. One of Apple's competitors flew a banner over the crowd telling them that it had jobs and profits waiting for them.

Another variation is to fly over beaches, rock concerts, sporting events, extreme games, or any other venue that attracts your type of employee or customer. The purpose need not be limited to recruitment. You can promote a new product or service. You can ask a question. Or, you can use this technique as a tease for something to come later. Get creative with it!

Think about where your employees or customers are when they are not at work. Learn their demographics, their buying behaviors, their escapes, their pleasures, their hobbies, their interests; and then fly your message in their faces. There aren't many people who won't notice and read something trailing behind a low-flying aircraft.

# #19  Monica

Forgive me, but this name is now synonymous with *intern* (as well as with some other things that we will not sink to here). If you have not considered bringing in college students to work with your company on a trial basis, you are missing an incredible opportunity, and so are they.

At the extreme, some technology companies are actually recruiting talented, high-potential students without college degrees and growing their own. But, short of that, it is well worth the time and trouble to bring in interns, or co-ops as they have been called in many engineering schools, not only to get some training, but also to sample your wares. And that is where many companies miss the point.

This is not your way of finding slave labor and getting undesirable work done. Unfortunately, that is what happens to many interns. They obviously may not have the skills or experience to be doing high-level work, and there's nothing wrong with putting them on those projects you would like to see done, but that haven't made it to the top of the heap (see "Wish List"), but a better option is to assign them as project assistants to high-level employees. Regardless of the assignment, if you want to get the maximum benefit out of an internship, approach the experience as a test drive and a recruiting tool, not as cheap help.

Even if the work the interns are doing borders on the mundane, you can still make sure that they enjoy the experience (not in the Monica way). Use the ideas in this book to make sure that they have some fun, that they have mentors, and that they leave wanting to come back. Otherwise, just hire a temp. Your company can do without the bad PR on campus. Students talk!

Once you have done that, create some incentives for these interns to return to you full time (see "Bridge Over Troubled Waters," for example). Involve them in some enjoyable tasks, like working on a special event or party. Give them an orientation to the rest of the company for a few days so that they can see it all and envision how they might fit in and contribute after they graduate.

Assign a mentor to show them the ropes, to invite them to interesting meetings, and to keep in touch with them when they are back in school.

Many of the boomerang strategies in this book, which are designed to get former employees to return, will also work for interns. Treat them the same way. Keep them on your mailing list, invite them to company events, send them job postings. The bottom line is, don't lose touch with them during the other nine months of the year (see "Missing You"). Assign a linkage person, preferably their mentor or peer host. Offer them staff support and company resources for their school projects, or let them use your company in their case studies or other research projects. Again, consider them on sabbatical or on leave of absence, and get them back. That's when you really get a return on your intern investment.

The other benefits of a successful Monica program are numerous. Not only do you get some work done that might not otherwise get done, but you also get good public relations, if the experience is good. Make your interns ambassadors for your company. Students talk to students. Make them eligible for your "Bird Dog" bonus. (See "Bird Dog Biscuits.")

You are planting the seeds for growing future employees, and you can try before you buy. And don't forget to send out press releases to their school and hometown newspapers announcing their new assignment with you (see "All the Right Places").

You will know quite quickly whom you want and whom you don't. You will see what kind of work habits your interns have, their attitude, their flexibility, if they fit your culture, and all the other variables that you can rarely assess during an interview. In addition to being a powerful recruiting and public relations tool, an internship is also a real-time, real-life bozo filter (see "Bozo Filter").

Finally, do not assume that you have to rely on formal college co-op or intern programs. Create your own! If you have a major project that requires a significant number of hours of research, data collection or entry, or any other trainable task, go to your local college, university, or tech school and post the project opportunity on the placement office bulletin board or some other high-traffic area (student centers, cafeterias, dorms, fraternity and sorority houses, etc.). Or, use these assignments to develop a positive relationship with key professors. You may be able to rely on them for full-time, high-quality candidates later. As you can see, the benefits of an intern program are numerous and well worth the effort.

# #20 Are You Talking to Me?

Who writes your ad copy? And, whom are they writing it for? Ads and agencies are not cheap, so don't waste your money being generic. Ask yourself, whom am I talking to? Then, identify your targets' values and styles and follow their lead. If this means being irreverent, be it. If it means being humorous, be it. If it means being flat-out stupid, be it!

What's your objective, anyway? Don't be afraid to shock people, or maybe even offend them. If this achieves your objectives, you can apologize all the way to the bank. You're running a business, not a political party.

Most advertising agencies and design firms are known for trying to please the person writing the check. Unfortunately, that's usually some staid old CEO, or, even worse, a whole team of them. What do they know about what is cool to someone a generation or two younger than they are?

Look at the leaders in retail communication who have a targeted message for a target audience. A good example is Volkswagen, whose commercials were masterful at the art of selling cars to Generation X. Another one is The Gap, which communicates almost entirely without words. Or Nike. I am sure you can think of many others.

What is the common denominator of these successful marketers? They communicate in the style and method most suited to their intended listeners, not the way you'd like to see it in your annual report (see "Lose the Legalese"). Also find out if your demographic markets (both customers and candidates) are more prone to use and respond to direct mail, television, radio, the

Internet, the telephone, or something else, then dedicate a higher percentage of your resources to that medium.

Companies like Netscape and Cisco Systems advertise in places where their kind of people hang out. Cisco has linked to the Dilbert Web site, and right before the Super Bowl, they advertised on Boston's leading electronic city guide. Cisco also buys time on sites like TravelQuest, the reservation service. Software lets Cisco read the URLs of Web surfers and match them to outfits they like to recruit from (such as competitors 3Com and Bay Networks). It then paints a banner with a link to the company's job page.

One way of learning where to go is to conduct a focus group. Not only is it a great source of information, but it can also serve as a powerful public relations tool. And then, test your marketing and recruiting communications with a focus group that represents your target market, and get their reactions. It's a lot cheaper to scrap or modify an ad before you run it than it is to find out after the ad has been run that it had no effect, or a negative one. At that point, the ad agency and the media already have your money.

## #21 Bird Dog Biscuits

Rewarding people, and not just employees, for referring new hires to your company is both economical and effective. If you think about how much a search firm charges for finding warm bodies (20 to 30 percent of the first year's compensation), doesn't it just make sense to be willing to reward other people you know for doing the same thing? Many organizations, particularly technology-based ones, are paying hundreds to thousands of dollars to successful bird dogs, which is a bargain when you consider what these organizations are getting. Over 40 percent of Microsoft's new hires come from employee referrals. Nearly 65 percent of Silicon Graphics' new hires begin as referrals from current employees.

Statistics also show that employees will generally refer higher-quality candidates than other sources because their reputation is on the line as well. Similarly, most people with whom you do business and with whom you have developed a relationship (vendors, customers, suppliers, etc.) will also be judicious in the types of people they refer. Current employees and others with whom you do business can be your best recruiters (and screeners) because they already know and understand what you do, your values, your culture, and all those intangibles that cannot be as effectively communicated in an ad or through other traditional sources. In any event, isn't it the job of human resources to screen and select the best people? This just improves the odds for them.

In fact, one of the best times to ask employees for referrals is when they are newly hired. Not only do they want to please their new employer, but they just left another organization for some reason, and there are probably others in the new hire's circle of influence who may also be interested in improving their lot in life. This isn't limited to former coworkers; it could also include spouses, friends, mentors, and many others. (Just as an aside, if you ask for references, you know that they are always going to speak well of the candidate, so instead of just asking them for their input, see if they are looking for a job, too.)

Most companies require more than just a warm lead or a name. In some, bird dogs are expected to talk with the candidates before the interview to tell them about and sell them on the company, to host them during their visit (also see "Birds of a Feather"), to talk with them afterward to see if they have any questions or concerns, and finally to talk with them after an offer is extended to help close the deal.

Another important twist on this concept is in how you pay the bonus. In order to improve and reward retention as well as hiring, some organizations pay the bird dog bonus in installments. In other words, the bird dog might get half of the bonus on the date of hire and the other half six months to a year later, or some other variation of the installment plan. This gives the bird dog (friend) a stake in keeping his or her referral with the company long enough for you to realize a return on your investment. It encourages an ongoing, supportive buddy system. It also creates an incentive for the bird dog to stick around because if the bird dog leaves, she or he loses too. Both the new employee and the referring employee must stay if the refer-ring employee is to get paid in full.

One company actually pays the bird dog a second bonus after one year if the employee he or she referred receives an excellent performance review. (Also see "Headhunter Hostage Pay.") There are even some companies that pay different amounts based upon the level and difficulty of the position(s) to be filled. In other words, for "commodity" talent, you might pay a few hundred dollars, but for "rare" talent, it could be thousands. Again, if you compare the cost of traditional sourcing, this is an obvious bargain.

There are also companies that will pay a special bounty for steal-ing talent from the competition. In fact, some are particularly inter-ested in stealing the competition's top internal recruiters, because this not only improves the company's recruiting ability, but also cripples the competition's recruiting efforts for a while.

Lastly, some organizations enter referring employees into a draw-ing (the more referrals hired, the more entries in the drawing) and periodically award something really grand, like a new car. MCI WorldCom gave away a brand new Porsche and was even smart enough to display the car in the lobby where everyone had to walk by it every day.

## #22 Bait the Hook

Like "Bird Dog Biscuits," this idea involves paying a bonus, but in this case the bonus is paid to the employee being hired, and for a different purpose. When you are fishing around and trying to steal someone from his or her current employer—i.e., the "passive" job seeker—compensation is usually a larger factor in the person's decision to jump ship.

However, no organization wants to find itself paying people way out of the competitive market range just to get them in the door. One solution is to do what professional sports teams have done for years for critical talent. They pay such people a signing bonus, or, in this case, a "hiring" bonus, to come to work for them. It is a one-time, lump sum payment upon hire.

This is a win-win because it has greater short-term impact and value to the recruit. Paying someone $10,000 in a lump sum now has a much higher perceived value than paying her or him $192 per week for fifty-two weeks, and it costs the employer much less in the long run because the employee's actual base salary is kept within a competitive range.

Additionally, since many benefits are also calculated as a function or percentage of compensation (such as life insurance, disability insurance, pension contributions, etc.), these costs are also kept proportionately lower, while your base compensation expense remains competitive with the market.

Finally, as was mentioned in "Bird Dog Biscuits," you may not want to pay the entire hiring bonus all at once at the time of hire. In other words, as with the bird dog bonus, you want to foster retention as well as reward recruitment. However, in this case, you do not want to lose the present value effect, so pay at least half or more of the bonus at the time of hire, and the remainder at a later date.

# WeIRD IDeAS FOR THE CARE AND FEEDING OF ToDAY'S TALeNT

## aka RETENTION

*Many human resources people and other managers claim that they cannot hold onto talent because they cannot afford to pay people enough to make them stay. That's not only a cop-out, but it also demonstrates a lack of creativity and understanding of the talent market. Even if people tell you they are leaving for more money, most of them either are just saving face or saving you the embarrassment of the cold, hard truth, or just want to get out with minimal hassle. They also figure that if you don't already know what the problems are that are causing people to leave, then that's all the more reason to jump ship. Or, worse*

*yet, they can't articulate why they are leaving, but they do know that it's worth taking a chance on a new employer if the money is at least as good because the environment couldn't be any worse.*

*So, if it isn't money, what is it? It's all those things you tried to convince them you were when you were wooing and recruiting them: "This is a fun place to work." "People are our most valuable asset." (yuk) "We believe in training and development." "We're one big happy family." Need I go on?*

*If you still think retention is mainly about money, find out how much it is costing your competition to get people to leave you. That's called your "poach rate." If your poach rate is less than 20 percent, it ain't the money, honey! People who love their work, love their boss and love their company don't leave unless the offer is coming from the Godfather.*

*Every study ever done on turnover has proved that the top reason why people leave one employer for another is always some variation on, "My boss was a jerk!" It may be cloaked in terms like communication or leadership style or lack of flexibility or trust, but it doesn't take a Ph.D. to make the translation.*

*A final thought: If you think that the problem in keeping good people is due to a pervasive lack of loyalty, that people today will jump ship at the drop of a hat, yada yada yada, why aren't all these turncoats coming to you? Why is this lack of loyalty only benefiting your competitors? Successful companies seldom lack for job applicants. Southwest Airlines averages forty applicants for every person hired. Silicon Graphics hires thousands of people annually, but receives tens of thousands of résumés from which to choose. Start doing some of the wacky things in this book, and you may just see a return to the good old days.*

## Gimme Three Words

**# 23**

One of the first things a company should do before developing a mission statement, guiding principles, or core values statement is to poll its people. You may want to believe that yours is a progressive, trusting, caring, and responsive organization, but writing it down in a document doesn't make it so. Find out first.

You need not create a long, sophisticated survey. Just ask everyone to write down three words that would describe whatever it is you are trying to define, such as your culture, your core values, your human resource philosophy, or your management style. In fact, by limiting their responses to only three words, it forces people to prioritize and identify the most prevalent and powerful descriptors.

For example, in one of my programs about how to attract and retain high performers, I ask attendees to write down three words that describe their recruitment process from the perspective of the person being recruited. Some of the words I have heard are *slow, structured, inflexible, bureaucratic,* and *difficult.*

Then I ask the attendees if these are the kinds of words they would like people to use to describe their organization's culture. The answer is obviously no. Good or bad, however, your recruitment process communicates your culture to outsiders; if it is slow, overly structured, inflexible, and bureaucratic, they are going to assume that your company is also slow, overly structured, inflexible, and bureaucratic, and you are not going to attract people who prefer to function in an entrepreneurial, action-oriented, or high-performance environment.

Once you have compiled all the lists of descriptors, look for the most commonly repeated words and look for common themes. This will tell you what the "shared values" in your organization are. Then, share them with everyone—the good and the bad.

When a large, *Fortune 100* former employer of mine conducted a similar perception survey, the number one overriding value expressed was integrity. Everyone knew it and felt it, but few people knew that everyone else knew it and felt it. Once this common response was shared with everyone, it reinforced everyone's pride and confidence in working for a company with a culture of integrity. And now they could also articulate it to others.

The results from this simple perception survey can be used in numerous ways, including creation of a shared values statement, development of new initiatives for change, and preparation of an orientation tool for new employees. In a small group setting, it can be the basis for further discussions and to identify strengths and weaknesses as part of a strategic planning effort. In any event, whether you do it in writing, which allows for anonymity, or in a workshop setting, which sparks discussion, it is a wonderfully simple yet powerful exercise.

## #24 Come on Down!

This was originally called an open meeting policy, but I prefer to call it a privilege because policies are intended to restrict behavior rather than encourage it. (See "Mirandas.") (Just for your information, the Greek root of the word *policy* is *polis*, which is the same root as the word *police*). The basic premise of an open meeting privilege is twofold. First, it requires that there be a mechanism in place that allows people to find out what meetings are scheduled and when and where they are. Second, it implies that these meetings are open to anyone who wants to attend and can attend.

One of the first companies to successfully introduce the concept of open meetings was Wang. At the time, Wang was already known for its culture of openness and trust, and as a natural part of that culture, it saw the value of not just allowing but *encouraging* people to know what was going on beyond their job description or even their department. Wang did not want people working in silos (see "Silo Destruction").

Obviously there are some parameters that you must establish and define for your organization, such as travel restrictions, prioritization of other duties, whether attendees are observers only or if they can participate, if there is a limit on how many people can attend at one time, and if so, is it on a first come, first served basis, and so forth.

There are several key objectives. One is to make people a part of the bigger picture. There is a tendency for individuals and departments to develop organizational tunnel vision when they are not exposed to anything outside their own areas. In other words, they see and relate to only the narrow objectives and consequences of their personal section of the organization (also see "Silo Destruction" and "Mind Your Own Business!").

Another objective is personal development. If someone in operations wants to know more about marketing strategies, what better way than to sit in on a marketing meeting? If a sales representative wants to learn more about the technical side of the product or business, why not allow him or her to sit in on a tech service meeting? The possibilities are endless.

A third objective is to kill the grapevine. Numerous studies have confirmed that the number one source of information in most organizations is the grapevine (aka, water cooler talk, coffeepot talk, etc.). However, those same studies have also shown that the number one *preferred* source of information is the source itself (i.e., management, the owners, etc.). The open meeting privilege opens these sources of information to the masses and eliminates the value and the validity of the grapevine (also see "Heard It Through the Grapevine").

Finally, it can reduce resistance to change. For example, when working on sensitive and difficult change projects such as performance management systems or other human resource initiatives that will affect everyone personally, we publish the names of the members of the task force, as well as our objectives and the dates, times, and locations of our meetings, and invite people to sit on the sidelines if they are interested.

At the first meeting(s) there are usually a handful of people. Once they see that there is nothing to hide, and that the meetings are actually rather boring, we rarely see anyone again. Word gets out pretty quickly on something like this. Just for insurance, we post our minutes on the bulletin board after each meeting to continue to let every-one know what is going on.

Eventually, when it comes time to roll out the new program, it is next to impossible for people to object or resist, because they had every opportunity to be heard long beforehand. In fact, if they act sur-prised, they look rather stupid, since they are admitting that they were oblivious to the opportunity of knowing what was going on all along.

One of the ironies of the open meeting privilege is that the more you open up the organization, the more trust develops, and ulti-mately no one feels a need to exercise the option. That is exactly what Wang experienced. Its culture was already built on high trust, so the privilege was rarely exercised.

# #25 Mirandas

You have the right to remain silent. You have the right to an attorney. You have rights, period. Let's take that policy thing a step further. Have you ever wondered about some of the stupid policies that you have encountered? Like a "no return" policy at a store? In other words, we'll be glad to take your money, but we ain't givin' it back! Or, how about the stupid seat back rule on airlines? It's not exactly a La-Z-Boy Recliner. Tell me whose life was ever saved in a plane crash because someone else's seat back was in its full upright and locked position. That two inches is a law! This could be another whole book.

So, let's turn the traditional policy concept upside down. Instead of creating policies that restrict and police behavior, how about some policies that set people free and empower them, or anti-policies? We have seen the beginning of some real-life examples of this idea in the movements for a "Passengers' Bill of Rights" for air-line victims (oops, I mean customers), or a "Patients' Bill of Rights" for the medical "industry."

If you take that idea and apply it to your organization, you could create a Customer's Bill of Rights, or an Employee's Bill of Rights. For example, the customer has a right to return merchandise for any reason, as long as it came from your store. Or, the employee has a right to satisfy a customer without going through multiple levels of bureaucracy while the customer waits. Here is a policy from the Ford Motor Credit Company that is to be visibly posted in Ford dealerships where customers can see and read it before making their buying decisions:

### CUSTOMER BILL OF RIGHTS

- You have the right to honest information when you request it, without evasiveness.

- You have the right to clear and thorough explanations of all financing/purchase details.

- You have the right to receive copies of all documents signed.

- You have the right to prompt and efficient service with genuine concern for your time.

- You have the right to choose which products and services you purchase.

- You have the right to expect the value of products and services to be equal to or exceed the purchase price.

- You have the right to courteous and professional treatment at all times.

- You have the right to be invited to buy without feeling pressured.

- You have the right to expect us to keep our promises to you.

The Ritz-Carlton Hotel empowers *all* employees to spend thousands of dollars in their efforts to satisfy a customer complaint or resolve a problem without getting someone else's approval. No, the privilege is not abused. Yes, there are instances where honest mistakes are made, but those rare occurrences are considered ongoing training, and because of the open communication and intent of the "policy" at the Ritz, they become learning experiences. Nordstrom department stores have been known to take back merchandise that they don't even sell!

Another anti-policy could be to ensure that employees have the right to information or answers to legitimate questions, no matter how sensitive or politically incorrect they may appear.

The key to "weird policies" is to look at everything you enact and ask whether it restricts behavior and freedom or enhances them. There is always an inverse relationship between the amount of trust and the number of policies an organization has. The less trust there is, the more policies there will be. Which kind of organization is yours?

## #26 Heard It through the Grapevine

As was touched on in "Come on Down," the grapevine is relied upon heavily in many organizations, particularly those in which there is little trust or communication. So, why not create your own grapevine? Since people prefer to get their information from the source, have your CEO, or whoever is the source of the latest information, put together a message that is to-the-point, nonsugarcoated, honest, and current, which people can access from anywhere, preferably on voicemail. Why voicemail? Because it has a voice! E-mail is fine for impersonal and generic information dumping, but there is still a place for hearing someone's voice and emotion, and this is it.

I remember when one of my clients was in the process of shopping for venture capitalists and on the brink of an initial public offering. This is the type of activity that will set the grapevine on fire. As the CEO, the CFO, and other members of the leadership team were traveling around the country, courting venture capitalists, making presentations, and trying to shape the company's future, the CEO recorded a very candid and personal message almost daily for anyone within the company to access, letting everyone know how the process was going, what the frustrations were, and particularly how it could affect employees.

The most important messages were those in which the CEO had nothing to report. What? Why would he do that? Because whenever there is a lack of information or communication, the grapevine will fill the void, and this is never good. No news is good news when it comes from the CEO. No news is bad news when it comes from the grapevine.

The CEO would actually say something like, "There really isn't anything new to report at this time, but rather than keeping you all hanging, I just thought you should know that we will be visiting so and so tomorrow, and that we will let you know when there is anything new, good or bad. Thanks for your patience and have a great day!"

The dial-up grapevine does not have to be used only for big issues. It can also be used to announce events, to share current trends in the industry that could affect the company, or for anything else that may be of general interest to the masses. That's the key.

Conversely, you can also set up an incoming grapevine. Instead of just giving information to people, create a vehicle that they can use to give you information, both bad and good. For example, at Barton Protective Services in Atlanta, Georgia, an employee can call a hotline to report violations of company values. This type of vehicle can prevent some huge problems down the road without involving outsiders. Why do you think we have to have federal laws to protect whistleblowers?

Just don't fall into the trap of sharing only good news or spreading corporate manure. If you do, not only have you wasted your time and theirs, but the manure you are spreading will just fertilize the grapevine, when your real objective is to kill it.

# #27 Mind Your Own Business!

This idea may sound radical to some, but there is a generally increasing movement toward something called "open book management," which will become the norm, and ultimately a requirement for any organization that wants to attract and keep top talent. It's making your business everyone's business.

"Mind Your Own Business!" goes beyond sharing information on a "need to know" basis; it moves it to a "want to know" level. In other words, if someone *wants to know* what the company spends on equipment, supplies, or other business expenses, he can get it. If someone wants to know what the strategic plan is, she can see it. The more high performers you hire, the more "nosiness" you are going to have. This is not only normal but healthy.

More and more companies today want people to perform and act like business partners—i.e., to be willing to eat, sleep, breathe, and live their work—so it is rather hypocritical, and subsequently ineffective, to think you can exclude them from legitimate big-picture business information at the same time.

To quote George Gendron, editor-in-chief of *Inc.* magazine, "I think the most significant business management trend in the coming age is open book management." He says that in its simplest form, open book management is based upon three precepts:

1. Companies need to share all of their important financial and operating information with all of their employees all of the time.

2. Nobody will understand the information, so you have to train them. You have to run "economic and business literacy programs" within your company.

3. You have to increasingly find ways to tie all of your compensation within your company into your financials so that a greater and greater percentage of your compensation is incentive-based, exactly the way it is for an owner, i.e., based upon business results.

According to Jendran, open book management is the only significant management trend to come along in our lifetime that was invented by practitioners. It wasn't invented in academia; it didn't come from the Harvard Business School or from consultants. It came from the front line, and was popularized in Ricardo Semler's best-selling book *Maverick: The Success Story Behind the World's Most Unusual Workplace*. Open book management is more than just a bundle of techniques. It's here to stay. It represents a profound change in the way we look at business and capitalism in its purest form.

For example, at Whole Foods Market in Austin, Texas, not only is the CEO's salary capped at ten times the average store worker's pay, but employees can see anybody's gross pay. Now, that's open book! If you have nothing to hide, you have nothing to fear. If you're doing things right, you can do the right thing.

# #28 Family Day

Since family values and work/life balance have become a major concern for many people, why not recognize that you have hired family men and women and that the more their significant others feel that they are "in the loop," the more understanding and positive they may feel about sacrificing their partner to the company (also see "Bribe the Bride"). One way of doing this is to have an open house or reception for employees' families, friends, or whomever else they include in their nonwork lives. You may even find a new recruit in the process.

One company that tried a variation of this idea ("Bring Your Parents to Work Day") was Organic, a New York City Web design and e-services firm. Roughly 125 parents spent half a day learning what their Web-obsessed kids actually do for a living. The parents first participated in a sort of talk show, during which they did their best to explain what their children do. Then the parents were told what their kids really do, and why.

Family day can be done departmentally or organizationwide. In fact, conducting departmental open houses allows other employees to drop in and see what other people in the company are doing (see "Silo Destruction"). And, as always, don't forget to have food and beverage, and maybe some kind of logo gift or other fun memorabilia. It's a generous way of advertising. They get a gift and you get your name out there in all kinds of other venues.

# #29 Trinkets and Trash

Why is it that even malcontents and nonloyalists want a logo coffee mug? It never fails. Introduce a new mouse pad or coffee mug or T-shirt with your logo on it, and suddenly everyone is a devotee.

Rather than try to figure this out, why not take advantage of this logo mania? You can either give things away or you can sell them. Another way of putting it is, they can earn it or they can buy it.

Trinkets and trash are particularly valuable and useful in highlighting or announcing a current theme, issue, challenge or victory and making it visible and trendy. By putting the latest "thing" on a T-shirt (or some other form of "Trinkets and Trash"), you can create a splash that everyone wants to be a part of. It's something fresh and new, and no one wants to be left out.

Having a variety of merchandise allows you to use this merchandise as a recognition vehicle, as a campaign promoter, or just to stock the company store. What? You don't have a company store? You do now! Look at how much people will pay for merchandise with logos like Disney or Nike or sports teams on it. Set up a room or a showcase or even a catalogue that has as many trinkets and as much trash as you can handle. The buyers are paying you to advertise!

The types of items you can use are endless. You can get ideas from any number of personalized merchandise companies. Or, bring your ideas home from trade shows and professional conference exhibitors. You know, those places you go for professional development and come home from with bags full of junk looking like an overaged "Halloweenie"!

Coffee mugs, mouse pads, stress balls, T-shirts, rulers, pens, highlighters, lapel pins, buttons, tattoos, hats, watches, rings, sticky notes, sunglasses, golf balls, markers, tees, towels, flashlights, candy, beer mugs, scratch pads, note cubes, letter openers, pillboxes, sewing kits, coasters, clocks, refrigerator magnets, key rings, luggage tags, calculators, tools, calendars, umbrellas, coolers, Frisbees, sun visors, stuffed toys, paper clip holders, seat cushions, first-aid kits, and don't forget a tote bag to put it all in! Need I go on? OK, so I've been to a few trade shows too.

## #30 Personal Space

When you buy a new car, one of the first things you do is to settle in by organizing the interior with your own radio and seat settings, your own set of creature comforts, and whatever else you can do to make it yours. It is no different for other places and spaces that people must occupy for extended periods. In addition to personalized job titles, allowing people to personalize their little corner of the world of work (i.e., their cubicle or other workspace) may be even more important and have more of an impact.

I remember the time (and this may still be the case in some organizations) when people's offices, furniture, and fixtures were actually a function of a formalized point system that assigned a relative value to each job. If you were a supervisor, you had a steel desk. If you were a manager, you had fake wood. If you were a director or vice president, you had real wood. This formula also determined whether you had a window or a corner office, and even the type and size of chair you sat in. It didn't matter that I am 6'3" and have a bad back; I was a supervisor, and therefore I had to survive sitting in a steno chair that barely went above my butt for almost three years until I got promoted to manager and could get something a little more ergonomic. (Do I sound bitter?)

Heck, we even had corporate plants! If you wanted to bring in your own little piece of greenery for your office, not only did it have to be approved, it had to be quarantined for a period of time to make sure that it wouldn't contaminate the corporate flora. Even the artwork was purchased by a corporate art committee. And, to make sure it was equal opportunity artwork, it was rotated throughout the headquarters on a predetermined scheduled basis, so everyone could love it or hate it for an equal amount of time. Gimme a break!

Anyway, now that most people have been relegated to cubicles or some other variation of limited personal space, it is even more critical that we give them liberty instead of death by allowing them some freedom of expression within their work area. Whether it is plants, paint, lights, decorations, stuffed toys or some other paraphernalia, let them be.

Some organizations provide not only the freedom, but even the resources to tailor personal work spaces. When Xperts Inc., an information technology consulting firm, moved to new digs just outside of Richmond, Virginia, they gave their people $1,500 each to cover the cost of "decorating" their new spaces. The company believed that this could contribute to a higher degree of loyalty, which it did. It just makes sense that if people can create their own corner of the world at work, they will feel better about being there. The deeper they dig in, the less likely it is that they will dig out.

# #31   1 + 1 = 3

You're seeing more and more of them. They're called strategic alliances. Whether it's a fast-food restaurant inside a convenience store or a bank inside a grocery store, companies are starting to merge products and services for mutual benefit, and hopefully financial success and synergy (i.e., 1 + 1 = 3, or "the whole is greater than the sum of the parts"). Remember the yin/yang!

You can do it too. Look for organizations and services that your employees and your customers tend to use. It may be worth doing a demographic analysis to find the biggest pockets of buying behaviors, but you can probably get a pretty good idea of what would and would not work if you just ask.

In the workplace, there could be a gourmet coffee bar run by a franchise, or a health club brought in-house as a satellite facility from a larger, established spa, or even a third-party, established day care center on site. Or, if a lot of your employees have pets, you might develop an alliance with a pet grooming and boarding service to set up a facility on the company grounds. This is especially useful for employees who have to do a lot of overnight travel for the company. Or, they might just like to be able to visit Fido or Fifi during the day—kind of like pet day care.

When you turn this idea toward the customer (both internal and external), the options become quite diverse and plentiful. One way to get a quick reading on what types of ancillary services and products your customers would want to buy is to see who wants to buy your database. Given the rampant sale and use of customer databases, you can rest assured that the demographers know your customers and their buying habits better than you do.

Even if you aren't in the market to add new products or services to your own mix, you may still want to develop strategic alliances with other organizations that already target the same market that you do. You will both immediately increase the size of your prospect list with high-quality leads and be able to market yourselves as being more responsive to your existing customer bases. Win-win-win is the mission of "1 + 1 = 3."

## #32 Rock Me, Baby!

This idea taps into the language of music, which is particularly alluring to a lot of young up and comers. Current literature tells us that a significant number of young technology workers are also closet musicians, audiophiles, and groupies in their nonwork life. Not only do they attend a lot of concerts (rock, alternative, new age, Christian, etc.), but many of them are actually in bands.

One obvious way to tap into their world is to sponsor a concert or to advertise wherever concerts are taking place (see "Lucy in the Sky With Diamonds" or "All the Right Places"). At least start putting your recruiting advertising on *their* radio stations, not yours (see "Are You Talking to Me?").

You can even take this a step further. Find out who the closet musicians at your company are and organize a jam session or a battle of the bands, or sponsor a talent show (see "Talent Show"). Free entertainment for everyone and catharsis for the band! You may eventually sponsor your own company band, which can perform at community events or other activities and provide opportunities for creative public relations. Another win-win.

Another idea is to charter a bus and sponsor a road trip to a popular concert or music festival. And remember, don't just invite your employees; invite their partners and even your ex-employees and recruits (see "Missing You"). If cost is an issue, don't worry about it. Attendees will gladly pay their way for a group road trip without the hassle or potential liability of driving. It's cheaper, safer, and more fun than going alone.

If you're still stuck on the need to justify it with corporate lingo, call it a "team-building" experience.

## #33 Show Me How to Keep the Money

As compensation and benefits plans get more flexible and more complicated, it becomes more and more difficult for people to make educated decisions on matters that affect their financial well-being and that of their families.

Many executives with deferred compensation plans, stock options, and other perks are given free financial planning, and have been for years. With more and more complicated and ever-changing compensation and benefits concepts now reaching almost every level of the organization, and with tax laws and investment vehicles constantly changing, why not help all your people maximize the value of their package by giving everyone professional financial advice?

There are many professional advisers who will provide these consultations at reduced group rates in the hope that they will expand their own client portfolio, generate new business, create goodwill, and get referrals for new business.

This advice idea can extend beyond the company compensation and benefit plan. With more people than ever playing the stock market and taking charge of their own investments and retirement planning, these kinds of services are indispensable (see "Special Services").

# #34 Will Work for Food

Although many companies have provided free coffee or maybe even sodas (aka pop, where I live) for a long time, others have started to realize the power of brain food (and I am not referring to health food here) as a workplace perk and productivity enhancer.

Even if you do not want to provide these things as standard fare, consider adding M&Ms, ice cream, Mountain Dew, and other so-called junk food to your list of periodic cuisine. In fact, if you do not want to make such luxuries standard, then find reasons for the occasional sweet celebration and make it special.

Maybe on a hot midsummer day, you can have a truckload of ice cream bars delivered for a mid-afternoon break. There are ice cream parlors that will deliver and set up a complete ice cream buffet with all the toppings at a very reasonable price, so employees can create their own ice cream masterpieces. CDW Computer Centers has free ice cream all summer long. Or maybe at the end of a long, tough project, you can have a junk food buffet. Get creative with it. An easy, fun way is to have a junk-food covered-dish event and have people bring in their favorite treats to create an entire smorgasbord of sinful indulgences.

Another option that is not only inexpensive but effective is to put a popcorn maker somewhere where everyone coming into the building can smell it. (Also see "Work Smells.") Even if you don't eat the popcorn, the smell is alluring. Most people associate the smell of popcorn with something festive. I guarantee you that it will become a popular snack item, as well. And those who may be more health-conscious than the average techie can also enjoy it without the salt.

# #35    Brainpower Inventory

This is nothing more than a formal survey of people's skills, knowledge and interests. People are more than job titles (also see "Talent Show"). This is a way to find out more about people, and to find additional ways to tap their unused skills for mutual benefit. They get to use and demonstrate their hidden abilities, and the company gets two talents for the price of one.

Rather than forcing people to find diversions off the job (see "Get a Life"), you can capitalize on the diversity of their brainpower internally through special assignments, developmental activities, and wish list projects (see "Wish List").

Perhaps you have an artist in your midst who can create graphics or visuals for your next annual report or provide artwork for your lobby or conference room.

Maybe you have people who are multilingual and can serve as interpreters or translators for foreign guests or in international correspondence. If you have ever paid a translator or hired a service to translate a letter into another language, you will quickly find out how valuable this person could be.

Recognizing the value of the whole person benefits both the individual and the organization. It allows people to blossom beyond their job description, saves the company money, and could even reduce turnover. In fact, just the inventory itself is an interesting document to share with everyone. It's simply amazing how people can work together for years and know little or nothing about one another beyond the job (see "Getting to Know You").

# #36    Cards for Everyone!

Even if you don't want people to make up their own weird titles (see "You Can Call Me Ray!"), at least think about giving everyone, and I mean everyone, business cards. You will be amazed at the pride people will feel and demonstrate when they have business cards. American Century in Kansas City, Missouri, has been doing this for quite some time.

A lot of the ideas in this book are intended to create ambassadors for your company, generate good public relations, and make people feel better about their work and their employer, and this is one of the easiest, cheapest ways to do it.

Whether you are the CEO or the mailroom coordinator (not clerk, please), you have numerous opportunities to give your organization positive exposure. In fact, those who would not ordinarily have business cards appreciate them the most. I'll never forget how excited a grocery store video department "clerk" was when she showed me her new nameplate, which said Video Department Manager. She called me over just to see it, and said that her husband took a picture of her wearing it.

At parties, meetings, shopping, and all sorts of other public forums, people always ask, "What do you do?", which usually means, "Where do you work?" For just a few bucks, you can give all your employees the ability to advertise and promote your company proudly by giving them their own business cards.

While you are at it, and before you go to the printer, this is the time to take a fresh look at your existing job titles and see if any of them may sound demeaning or irrelevant, and if they could be tweaked a little bit. Try to avoid titles like *clerk* or *trainee*; consider using *associate*, *representative*, *coordinator*, or *assistant* instead. People put a lot of stock in what they are called and how they are perceived by others. Titles and business cards represent both.

## #37 Wish List

Are there projects that you would love to see accomplished, but that just can't seem to make it to the top of the heap? Why not make a "wish list" of projects for each department that could be published and ask for volunteers to do them?

As an internal process, this cannot be done with insecure managers or micromanagers. It requires a high level of trust between the manager and the volunteer to prevent the manager from meddling or imposing more work on the volunteer to counter the extra time and effort he or she is putting into the project. Obviously people must be meeting the requirements of their current assignment before they volunteer for additional work elsewhere, unless you just want to transfer them.

As an external process, you can make the wish list available to colleges and universities for potential internships or special assignments (also see "Monica"). And don't forget your alumni. If you are practicing any of the boomerang strategies to get former employees back, this might be another enticement for them to return. Or they may just want to work on an assignment on a freelance basis for extra money and variety.

As is explained in "Get a Life" and "Brainpower Inventory," high performers have needs beyond their immediate job, and if you cannot fulfill them, someone else will—like a competitor. In addition, since there is no such thing as a career ladder anymore (it's more like a scaffold), many people have their own personal wish list, which may include changing jobs or specialties.

For example, you may have someone who is working on a degree in human resources and would love to work on a human resources project to satisfy a school assignment or just to prove what he can do. Or, you may have a technical person who may want to get outside more, perhaps in a sales or tech service role. The possibilities are endless, but if the work needs to be done, and you can't do it, and there are people already in your company who would like to do it, you're nuts if you don't offer them the opportunity. They're already on the payroll.

## #38 Firefighter's Hours

Although the concept of flextime is not a new one anymore, there are a few new twists that can add a little more flex and benefit your company at the same time.

Assuming a traditional forty-hour week, which is probably not the standard for most high performers, you can squash those forty hours into four days instead of five (i.e., four days of ten hours instead of five days of eight hours). This is a diluted version of firefighter's hours, where they actually live at the firehouse around the clock until they get their weekly hours in.

It is doubtful that many companies would want to push this compressed workweek concept to the point of having employees work forty hours straight, but going to a four-day workweek affords incredible flexibility and quality of nonwork life and can make all the difference between working for you and working for someone else who doesn't offer such a benefit. Over 25 percent of employees at Northern Trust in Chicago, Illinois, are on compressed workweeks, and that's in addition to the 25 percent who are telecommuters.

If your operation runs 24/7 (i.e., twenty-four hours a day, seven days a week), you have quite a few options with this. You can maintain your 24/7 coverage without additional staff, you can overlap the shifts for peak times, and you can offer a variety of four-day weeks, such as Monday through Thursday, Tuesday through Friday, Wednesday through Saturday, and so on. Modified firefighter's hours is really no more difficult to administer than the *normal* flextime arrangements already being used by many companies, and in fact may even be easier and more appealing to everyone.

Some companies have adopted a temporary, watered-down version of this idea called *summer hours* in which everyone works an additional hour on Monday through Thursday so that they can knock off at noon on Friday during the summer. This arrangement is always well received, but be prepared for it to open the door to requests to make it a year-round standard practice.

# #39  Galloping Gourmets

It's starting to look as if one of the common denominators in a lot of great ideas is food. In any event, this one also plays to the need for quality conveniences and lifestyle enhancers (also see "Special Services").

Eli Lilly is one of the first companies I was aware of that had a "take-out" service whereby employees could order a high-quality dinner-to-go from the company's well-staffed and highly skilled food service department. Others are quickly following suit. Valassis Communications of Livonia, Michigan, has a "Gourmet-to-Go" program, with meals that are ready to heat and eat. Exotic dishes like sushi, ginger-marinated chicken breast, or even fettuccine puttanesca are available to employees of Adobe Systems in San Jose, California, for just a few bucks an entrée. Employees at Xerox's corporate headquarters in Stamford, Connecticut, can also order take-out meals from the company cafeteria, as can employees of J. C. Penney's Plano, Texas, headquarters.

Ideally, employees could order a complete dinner earlier in the day for their family that would be hot or reheatable and would be packaged and ready to go when they were on their way out the door for home. This sure beats picking up a bag of fast food or ordering pizza again and again.

In fact, this would even let an employee who wanted to be a little sneaky and who got home before his or her mate to serve up the courses nicely presented on plates with garnishes and pretend that he or she was actually able to juggle work and home with ease.

In terms of cost, this can be paid for by the employees. If your cafeteria is run by an outside contractor, the contractor can generate additional revenues with such a service, since it is over and above the existing contract. And, if the contractor balks at the idea of preparing yet another meal, put the meal out for bids. That's the beauty of free enterprise and capitalism. There's always someone willing to fill a need if it is profitable.

Or, you could bring a respectable restaurant in-house to meet the need (also see "1 + 1 = 3"). Wal-Mart has McDonalds; the Radisson has TGIFridays; why can't your company do the same?

# #40  Food for Thought

Not food again! Yes, the easiest way to a techie's brain is through the stomach. Actually, this is true for most people. And as they say, there's no such thing as a free lunch, and this idea proves it.

Since time is so limited in most high-performance companies, and learning is so valued, why not combine lunch with learning? Every so often, schedule a guest speaker, a training video, or some other easy-to-swallow learning program to coincide with lunch and provide a simple box lunch or cold buffet that people can enjoy at the same time. We can learn and eat at the same time, thus getting double duty out of the same hours. (P.S. Seasoned trainers know that it is better to serve cold food if you want participants to stay alert and attentive. Hot, heavy foods tend to make people drowsy.)

Be sure to announce the program well ahead of time so that people don't make other plans or bring in their own lunch and have to miss it. Springing a lunch program on people at the last moment can quickly turn what is supposed to be a very positive event into a negative one. You don't want to hear, "But, I already brought my lunch!" or "But, I already made other lunch plans!" or "If only I'd have known, I would…."

In fact, it may be best to have your "Food for Thought" program on a predictable schedule, like the second Tuesday of each month, so that it can be anticipated, planned for, and well attended. Look in your local phone book or your neighborhood for businesses that would like to get exposure to your people in exchange for a free presentation, like self-defense, financial planning, child safety, etc. But be sure the presenters do not hard-sell anything during the program, or your people will never come back.

You do not always have to provide heavy, job-oriented content (also see "Irreverence and Irrelevance"). I've even seen companies offer dance lessons; bring in improvisational theater groups, stand-up comedians, fortune tellers, or tarot card readers; and provide all sorts of other out-of-the-box experiences during these programs. The list of topics is endless: golf tips and lessons, sailing, juggling, relationships, woodworking, gardening, personal grooming, etiquette, pottery, painting, travel, safety, auto maintenance and repair, glassblowing, genealogy, legal advice, and the list goes on.

If you need to provide more serious, job-content-oriented training, this same format can work quite well. However, you should probably make it a departmental or functional lunch if the subject is not of general interest. For example, if a software company agrees to come in and demonstrate how to use its program(s) more effectively, this would be of interest and value only to the people who are using that particular software program. It would be a mini-users conference.

In any event, the key here is to take advantage of the time that people would be using anyway to stuff their guts and offer two free-bies at the same time, i.e., food and learning. That's "Food for Thought."

# #41 Learning, Not Leaving

Most major companies have tuition reimbursement pro-grams and other ways to subsidize continuing education, but this idea came out of an organization that employs a lot of min-imum-wage, high-school-age and college-age kids, who normally would not be eligible for these kinds of benefits. The company's objective was not just to encourage education (use it or lose it), but to increase retention and reliability of employees in a traditionally high-turnover industry. It was perceived as a valuable benefit that employees would lose if they left the company.

The basis of this concept is to create an education "bank account" that increases in value the longer the employee stays with you. It is even better to tie the value of the account to the actual number of hours or amount of pay the employee has accumulated, which also rewards attendance. In other words, rather than tying the account to "time on the job," tie it to "hours worked." There's a big difference!

For example, you might put twenty-five cents per hour into the fund and make it accessible or vested after a certain number of months on the job with satisfactory performance. You can design the plan any way you want, but be sure your design is linked to the behaviors you need organizationally, such as retention, attendance, etc.

Also, be sure you give your employees periodic bank statements reflecting their account balance so that they can watch the balance grow, to encourage continued loyalty. You can also define what types of education are eligible under the program, unless you are ultra-liberal and don't care what your employees learn, as long as they stay with your company. It's extremely cost-effective either way.

# #42  Lose the Legalese

Why do people write one way and talk another, particularly at work? If you were walking down the hallway and ran into a coworker, would you stop and say, "Please be advised that all staff is hereby instructed to convene next Tuesday, April 5, at exactly 10 A.M. in Conference Room A to discuss the following: blabiddy blah, blabiddy blah…"? Of course not!

So, why do your memos have to sound this way? Because we have let lawyers rule the world, and we tend to guard every word we commit to writing. Eventually we start to think that this is the only safe and appropriate way to communicate. Wrong! There are numerous opportunities to "Lose the Legalese" and lighten up on the lingo.

The following memo is an excellent example. Read it and ask yourself if it would get *your* attention and pique *your* curiosity a little bit more than the standard shtick. Try to guess what this meeting is for:

---

**INTEROFFICE MEMORANDUM**

**To:**       Everyone

**From:**   Ed

**Subject:**  Opportunity—defined by Webster as follows:

   *1. A favorable time or occasion*

   *2. A good chance for self-advancement*

---

It isn't often that you are presented with a "win-win"/"can't lose" opportunity such as the one that I have the privilege of offering to you. You will meet new people, have time off from work (with no penalty), be treated to refreshments, find out things about yourself that you probably didn't know, and leave with a feeling of euphoria. In addition to these benefits, you will not gain weight, get in trouble with the law, have a hangover, or reduce your bank account.

It is with a great deal of pride and pleasure that I ask you to stop by my office, or give me a call, so I can advise you on attaining this state of euphoria.

Signed,

Ed

___

Have you guessed what the meeting is? It's the annual blood drive. Read it again. Do you see anything remotely illegal or inappropriate about this memo? No! And it caused people to think a little differently about the same old event, got a few chuckles in the process, and broke all records for the annual blood drive. After all, getting people to show up for a blood drive is half the battle.

This may seem like a simple thing, but once you open the door to this style of communicating, it not only makes the day-to-day drudgery a little more fun, but also starts to develop a culture of creativity. Even routine activities start to take on a new flair, and people feel a little more empowered and liberated to free their minds from false formality.

Believe it or not, you can even lose the legalese in your more traditional and formal "legal" documents. A case in point is the new employee handbook. If your company has a new employee handbook, there's a good chance it is very wordy, dry, and seldom read unless there is a problem. The lawyers will have you put tons of cross-references, hereinafters, heretofores, multiple tabs, footnotes, and all the other stuff that justifies their existence and ensures that no one can blame them for any future problems (or profits).

If you and your lawyers still want to have such a document to cover yourself later, that's fine. You can even have the employee sign it in blood. But don't expect a new hire to read it from cover to cover and retain anything, or walk away feeling good about your company's culture.

What follows is an employee handbook (called the Blue Book—because it's blue) that has lost the legalese. It is given to all recruits and new hires at Anixter Bros., Inc., a cable and wire company based in Skokie, Illinois. The whole thing is only twenty-four pages long with lots of white space and is small enough to fit in your shirt or blouse pocket. Not only is it read and understood, but it communicates volumes beyond the words. See if you agree.

---

**OUR PHILOSOPHY**

1. People come first.

2. Our word is our bond—we are reliable.

3. We are Serious about Service.

4. We cannot afford the luxury of a lousy day's business.

5. We want to be the best.

6. We are realists and we believe in candor.

7. We are accessible and easy to do business with.

8. We are aggressive—we are doers—we work hard.

9. We are often pleased but never satisfied.

10. We properly reward our people.

**OUR SPECIALTY**

We are serious about service!

To make a better than average profit, you've got to have a better than average business.

Since we don't have proprietary products, our service must be outstanding.

Service is a state of mind. To give exceptional service, our people must really care—and they must have the desire to do it right and do it now.

Service costs money. So, we expect to get paid very well for being sensational.

Our motto: SERVICE IS OUR TECHNOLOGY®!

### CUSTOMERS AND SUPPLIERS

Customers are not dependent on us. We're dependent on them.

They're not an interruption of our work. They're the purpose of it.

We're not doing them a favor by serving them. They're doing us a favor by giving us the opportunity.

Customers bring us their needs. It's our job to handle them profitably, for them and for ourselves.

Customers are our passport to success. Without them we can't get there.

*And at Anixter, we treat Suppliers as Customers.*

*(So, substitute the word "Suppliers" for "Customers" and reread the above.)*

### TRUTH

We tell the TRUTH to each other and to our customers and suppliers.

The whole story, not just part of it.

We don't stretch it, bend it, or avoid it.

And, if someone raises hell when you tell the truth…let them.

Just say it like it is.

*One little lie and you're a liar!*

**EXPRESS YOURSELF**

Think! Think often, think hard and then say what you think.

Feel! Have strong feelings and then express them.

And don't get mad when others do.

**ENTHUSIASM**

Enthusiasm is the greatest business asset in the world. It beats money and power and influence.

Enthusiasm tramples over opposition, storms its objectives, and overwhelms all obstacles.

Enthusiasm is Faith-in-Action—faith to remove barriers and achieve the miraculous.

Enthusiasm is contagious, so carry it in your attitude and manner. It will increase productivity, and it will bring joy and satisfaction to our people.

Enthusiasm brings results.

**CHANGE**

There is nothing so constant as change.

Everything must change to grow.

So we welcome change because—

Change = Growth = Opportunity

**STUFFED SHIRTS AND BIG SHOTS**

Don't call me Mr. or Ms. because—

Everyone's on a first name basis at Anixter.

Everyone.

If somebody calls you Ms. or Mr. _____, tell them that your name is Matilda or Alfred.

Let's grow BIG—but stay small like a family.

Without stuffed shirts.

### VICE PRESIDENTS AND MANAGING DIRECTORS

Vice presidents and managing directors are regular people who have experience and knowledge that you can use to help do your job better.

They have friends and contacts, can usually sell pretty good and are able to take on special projects. This gives you additional hands and feet. And, two heads are always better than one.

Anixter vice presidents work for you (not the other way around).

So use them!

### OUR CONTRIBUTION

Each one of us must pay for ourselves each day.

This allows us to have exceptional men and women working for the company.

Strive to promote sales, control costs and increase productivity each day.

After all, Anixter's business is your business.

### HIERARCHY

Hierarchy turns an organization into a pyramid.

Pyramids don't move, they just slowly crumble.

*Everyone should do what they do best.*

Our company deserves to have the best talent working on its biggest problems—or best opportunities.

So we will continually reshuffle our people (and their titles) to suit the needs of the company…

…without a hierarchy getting in the way.

### JOB DESCRIPTIONS

*(blank page)*

## ORGANIZATION CHARTS

*(another blank page)*

## LETTERS

We are opposed to letter writing as a form of business communication.

They're too slow, too cold, and they just don't get the job done.

We want eyeball to eyeball conversation.

Next best is the telephone.

Letters are OK for summing up actions decided at meetings, making commitments to goals.

And thanking people!

## PHONES

We make our own calls.

We answer our own phones.

We're never "in a meeting" or "busy."

And no one at Anixter ever asks,

*"Who's calling?"*

## FIRST CLASS

We entertain first-class, always.

To do this we must have *first-class profit*.

So, think *first-class*, be *first-class*, and let's make the necessary *profit* to keep this company a *first-class* place to work.

## EXPENSES

This company is your business home.

Live in it according to your lifestyle.

Just pretend that the company's money you are spending is your own. (It's your company.)

And write your expense account so it won't embarrass you when it's posted on the bulletin board.

## HIRING

We don't hire people.

We invite them to join our company and help us make it better.

## FIRING

We don't fire people.

We ask them to leave the company and help them go where they can be productive.

## PROMOTIONS & TRANSFERS

Three questions must be answered in this order:

**1.** Does the person want to do it?

**2.** Can they do it?

**3.** Will they do it?

Just one No…and it's "No!"

## CASH FLOW

More should come in each month than goes out.

## COMPENSATION

Pay the producers what they're worth.

Ask non-producers to improve, coach them for success, then address alternatives if they don't produce.

## OUR CLIMATE

We work for fun and money.*

We believe in an open book.

We put issues on the table, work them out, then get down to growing the business.

*Is there any other reason to work?

**MANAGING**

Lead!

...or follow

...or get out of the way.

**PEOPLE**

"People" is the first word in our business philosophy...and the last.

Our business—any business—is People.

If we take care of Our People, they will take care of Our Business.

---

Ironically, the pages that communicate the most are the ones with no words at all (i.e., Job Descriptions and Organization Charts) If you were interviewing with or being hired by a company with a handbook like this one, wouldn't you be pleasantly surprised?

These kinds of communication do more than just give information. They communicate your style, sense of humor, creativity, culture, and so on. Differentiate yourself and your organization. Lighten up and lose the legalese.

# #43 Special Services

As more and more companies try to attract employees who have a passion for their work, expecting them to sacrifice their personal lives in the process, there is a trend, out of necessity as well as luxury, toward blending work life with real life.

Even with "normal" jobs (remember the good old Monday-through-Friday, forty-hour workweek?), most people still have to sacrifice their minimal discretionary time on weekends and in the evening to get the necessary chores like dry cleaning, haircuts, car repairs, and other life essentials done on the fly.

A great way to add zest to your benefits package, to differentiate yourself from the competition, and to improve productivity as well is to bring as many personal services as possible in-house. The great thing is that the providers of most of these services are willing to come to you (free) because they can generate bulk business in one place.

For example, dry cleaners love to be able to pick up and deliver a ton of clothes in one place. All the employer has to do is to provide a closet or room where people can drop off and pick up their cleaning. The bags can have a number or the employee's name on them so that the dry cleaner doesn't even need to see or talk to the customer/employee. For special instructions, like spots or stains, a mere note in the bag will suffice. No downtime is needed.

Merck & Co., the New Jersey–based pharmaceutical firm, is a good case in point. Its employees can get on-site dry cleaning, oil changes, and fresh bread without ever leaving the office. Some companies have even started providing pet day care services so that employees can bring their pets to work. Cherokee Ford in Woodstock, Georgia, even has a beauty shop for waiters (automotive service customers who are waiting on-site for their cars) and employees. What a great way to cut down the perceived wait time!

The same kind of convenience can be provided for film processing, health and beauty services, manicures, car washes, shoe shines— the list goes on. I've even seen one company where the shoeshines are done without the feet in them. In other words, you drop off the shoes you want to be shined in a numbered or named bag and pick them up later, just like hotels do with the doorknob bags. Another company actually allows the shoeshine guy to roam the halls and offices, shining shoes wherever the feet are. He plops down his shoeshine box at your desk and does the job while you continue to talk on the phone or work at your computer. He's become a real fixture, and everyone loves him.

Even automobile dealerships and manufacturers are jumping on this bandwagon by providing on-site auto maintenance and repairs. They send a van or truck with a certified technician to your place of work or home, or even to a school or sporting event, and the technician changes your oil, tunes up your car, or does any number of other repairs while you do something else.

Acxiom Corporation, based in Conway, Arkansas, has an even grander approach. It has a concierge (actually two of them) who takes personal requests for just about any possible service—pet care, home mortgage sourcing, restaurant reservations, you name it! They'll even run errands for you.

Goldman Sachs offers free limo service for those who work late into the night.

California construction firm Granite Rock's fully paid health plan covers twelve massages a year. Amgen, the biotech company, has on-site car rentals and a shuttle to the airport. Going a step further, Valassis Communications of Livonia, Michigan, which produces newspaper inserts, has "Wheels-on-Loan," for employees whose cars are in the shop. Valassis also has a program called "You've Got It Maid" that offers discounts on maid services. JM Family Enterprises (a Toyota distributor), of Deerfield Beach, Florida, not only provides free haircuts and manicures, but even allows employees to use the company jet in emergencies!

Because of this trend toward making workplaces more livable, organizations are starting to look more like little cities or communities than like corporate ivory towers. For example, BMC Software of Houston, Texas, is like a city within a company, with a full-service gym with personal trainers, an indoor basketball court, a hairstyle salon, two restaurants, and a car wash.

Think about it. After all, people need a lot of these personal services in order to support their work life. If it weren't for work, they wouldn't have so much dry cleaning, or have to be so attentive to personal grooming details, or need pet care, or be putting so many miles on the car. Many of these ideas can be implemented very inexpensively if you bring in outside service providers. In fact, there are companies springing up from coast to coast that will "concierge" for you, like LesConcierges in San Francisco, or Circles in Boston, or Internet-based Best Upon Request, based in Cincinnati, Ohio.

And it doesn't really matter whether these "Special Services" are company-paid or employee-paid. Employees will gladly pay for these conveniences, because they would pay for the service anyway.

But now they can actually use their limited free time to be free! Offering these services is easy, it's cheap, and people are happier about staying at work because they can have their personal needs tended to at the same time. And now their "free" time is truly free.

# #44 Free Consultants

"Free Consultants" is an exercise that can be used to assess the customer- or employee-friendliness of your company. Let's start by looking at employee-friendliness. The original version is called "visit your company again for the first time." It is based on first impressions and fresh perspectives, something veterans of the company do not have.

Who can better critique your recruitment, selection, orientation, and other "first impression" processes than someone who has just experienced them firsthand? Do not restrict the critique to just content, which is also relevant, but extend it to the process itself (time requirements, dead time, difficulty, confusion, etc.).

If you hire several people over a short period of time, you can wait and ask them all to complete a questionnaire or survey anonymously, which may lead to more candor. Or, you can bring them together for a lunch or dinner discussion to function as a focus group and give their impressions and recommendations. Not only will you get great information, but you will also make a great first impression by asking your freshmen their opinion so early in their relationship with you.

Now, about "Free Consultants" for customer service. Just take the same approach, but with a mix of new customers and long-time loyal customers. This is quite a powerful exercise because (1) you are acknowledging your customers' importance to you, (2) you are demonstrating a sincere interest in continuous improvement, (3) your new customers can see and hear from your loyalists, who have more credibility than you do, and (4) you will get incredibly valuable information and insights on how to continue to be the best in your industry and market.

And, don't forget to reward these customers with some type of deep discount coupon for your products or services, and/or a freebie logo gift (also see "Trinkets and Trash"). Why pay a marketing research company thousands of dollars to be your surrogate in a process in which you have everything to gain by doing it yourself?

# WEIRD IDEAS FOR CHANGING YOUR COMPANY CULTURE

## aka FUN & GAMES WITH A PURPOSE & A PROFIT

*There's been a lot of talk about organizational culture these days, but very few decision makers seem to be able to grasp it, change it, or even influence it in real, tangible, positive ways. Organizational culture is one of those hard-to-define intangibles. It's kind of like the way a famous judge once defined pornography. He said, "I can't define it, but I know it when I see it!" Just think of culture as the unwritten rules of behavior—the way we do things here; how it feels to work here.*

*In any event, don't worry about defining it. Just make it work for you and your company. The issue isn't whether you have a strong or a weak culture. You could have a very strong culture, but it could also be working strongly against you. The key is to be sure that your culture supports your mission, your strategy, and your objectives, i.e., that it contributes to productivity, employee morale, and job satisfaction. One way to understand the importance and the impact of a strongly aligned company culture is to see it in the context of the "cycles of service," illustrated in Figure 4-1.*

*One of the pitfalls for many who try to change or improve their company culture is taking too long a view. Organizational cultures develop over time, and also take time to change. And, as the old adage goes, "How do you eat an elephant?...One bite at a time!" Here are some of the bites you can take today.*

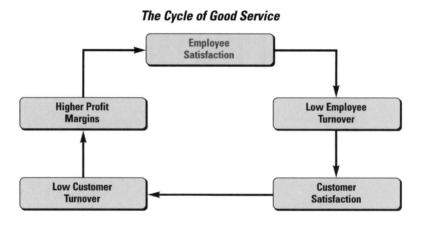

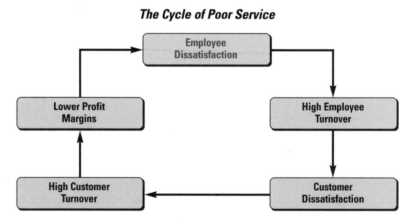

Figure 4–1 THE CYCLES OF SERVICE

# #45 Are We Having Fun Yet?

Work and fun are not opposites, nor should they be. In fact, having fun at work may require some work! That's why some companies make sure that fun is as much a priority as the real work is, by institutionalizing it. There is such a thing as productive fun, i.e., fun with a purpose. That is why I recommend forming a "fun committee."

Serving on a fun committee can be a fun endeavor, but the mission is a serious one. In fact, the committee should have a mission statement, such as, "Our mission is to ensure that everyone in the organization enjoys his or her time at work to the greatest extent possible, while achieving and maintaining maximum productivity and effectiveness."

Once the mission is established, the fun committee should be formed. It should meet at least once a month to discuss possible new themes, activities, or issues where it can inject some positive emotions around the seriousness of work. A book such as this one could be used as a thought starter. The committee could spearhead new contests or other initiatives that could keep the world of work at their organization fun and exciting.

One of the first companies to adopt a fun committee was Odetics, a California electronics company. In this spirit of fun, the CEO even donated his football pool winnings to buy smoothies for everyone (also see "Will Work for Food"). Other companies have also started to pick up on the fun committee concept, such as the Finova Group, a Phoenix, Arizona, company that provides capital to midsize firms, which calls its committee the Funovators for various social activities.

Ideally, the committee members should be temporary. Members should rotate off and new ones come on maybe twice a year or so. Keep people on long enough to produce and to get comfortable with the task and the team, but not so long that they become stale, bored, or frustrated with it. New brains mean new ideas!

One of my clients has an "employee of the month" program, with each month's winner automatically becoming a member of the screening and selection committee for the next period, while the person who has been on the committee the longest rotates off.

How you select your members can also be an exercise in creativity. Perhaps you can use a lottery, or make it an elected office, or even an honor. Whatever your method, make sure that being on the fun committee is as positive an experience as the environment the committee is trying to create for the organization at large.

## #46 Chain Letters

This is another form of sharing (also see "Show 'n' Tell" and "Share the Wealth of Knowledge"). People can send chain letters with personal recipes, poems, words of wisdom, or anything that others might find useful or interesting. With e-mail, this is being done whether you organize it or not. So why not institutionalize it for legitimate sharing and learning and take some credit for it?

For example, if a recipe chain letter produces enough responses, you could compile a company cookbook, sell it, and donate the proceeds to a charity. Or if you have a lot of artists or poets in your midst, you could do the same thing, but share the proceeds with the contributing writers or their designated charity.

There are many other chain letter ideas that are just for fun. However, avoid those that are financial. They can only lead to trouble and disappointment.

## #47 Dating Game

Believe it or not, this idea was first introduced in a doctor's office. It may not be for everyone, and particularly not for companies with strict antifraternization and/or antinepotism policies. Dr. Bob was one of those natural matchmakers who was always introducing patients to each other when he thought they would enjoy meeting. He would deliberately schedule single patients that he wanted to meet close together and would drop less-than-subtle hints along the way. He became known as "the singles doctor." And, not surprisingly, he was based in California.

Eventually his reputation as a natural matchmaker had been so firmly established, and his weirdness was so warmly received by his patients (he was booked solid), that he decided to formalize the service by offering patients the option of being included in a "singles book" in his lobby.

Along with your medical history questionnaire, insurance information, etc., he would give you a personal profile sheet that you could complete if you wanted to be listed in the book. No names or identifying information, such as phone numbers or addresses, was included, but any other information that you wanted to include was allowed, including sexual preferences, physical descriptions, hobbies, interests, religious beliefs, smoker or non, and so on.

Copies of these sheets were then put into three-ring binders and placed in the reception lounge along with the traditional magazines and other reading materials. Even for people who aren't looking for a mate, they make for intriguing reading and make the wait for the doctor a little more entertaining.

Others in the medical community, of course, reacted quite negatively, saying that this was unprofessional and was not the purpose for which they went to medical school. Yeah, right! Who should decide what the customer wants? The customer, of course! And if you don't want to participate, you don't have to. If you don't like the art, stay out of the museum.

Ironically, these same dissenting doctors' schedules were not nearly as full as Dr. Bob's, which may have been the real source of resentment. Better yet, Dr. Bob was always being featured in the media as a "unique doctor who truly cares about his patients." You can't buy that kind of advertising (see "All the Right Places," "Are You Talking to Me?" and "Customer Appreciation Days").

I don't know about you, but in today's social world, I'd much rather meet a prospective partner through my doctor than in a bar. Wouldn't you?

# #48 Graffiti for Good

After attending one of my Tapping Your Natural Weirdness sessions, Medrad (a Pittsburgh, Pennsylvania-based developer, manufacturer, and marketer of medical devices) came to the realization that they took themselves too seriously. As proof that they were on the high road to weirdness, in addition to many other weird initiatives, they formed a group called Wacky Wisdom Works (WWW for short). The goal was to bring some fun into Medrad (also see "Are We Having Fun Yet?").

The conference room in which WWW held its meetings and planned its events (aka the Duquesne Room) was scheduled to be demolished for renovation. So, looking for an opportunity in the crisis, the company came up with the idea of charging "two bits for your two cents worth," which meant that for a quarter, you could go into the room and make a graffiti statement, paint pictures, leave silly slogans, knock holes in the wall, or do whatever made you feel better (see Figure 4-2). Figures 4-3 and 4-4 show the work in progress and

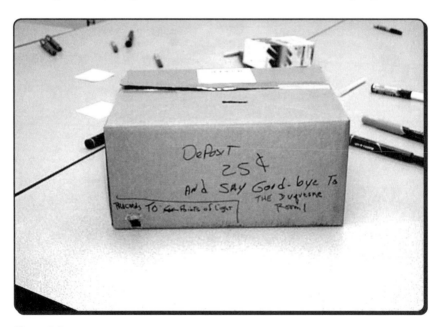

**Figure 4-2**

Figure 4-3

Figure 4-4

a final example of their handiwork, respectively. After all, the room was going to be history in a few days anyway.

All of the money raised through this cathartic exercise went to another committee called the Points of Light Committee, whose job it was to distribute the money to various charities.

Even if your company does not have a demolition project planned, you can still find a room somewhere that fills the bill. After all, if companies can afford to have in-house health spas, they can surely afford an empty room with markers, paint, and tools! In one company I visited, I saw a wonderful example of this theme that any company could use. This company has a conference room in which all the walls, from floor to ceiling, are made of dry-erase white boards. There are numerous markers in a rack attached to the wall, and people can just go nuts with their artistic expression and creativity.

Even better, this room is now perfect for brainstorming sessions and other meetings in which you need to draw or document as you go. It is also great for flowcharting because you don't need multiple pages all taped together—you can just keep on going around the room! And when you're done, you can easily wipe the whole room clean for the next bunch of crazies. Once again, fun can have a purpose and a side benefit too.

## #49 Hello, My Name Is . . . and I'm . . .

With the ever-increasing emphasis on diversity, freedom of choice, syndromes of the month, and all the other "I am unique" movements out there, there is also a correspondingly growing need for people to be able to identify and connect with others, find some kindred spirits, and validate their stations in life. This is rather oxymoronic, actually: Collective individualism!

In spite of this, there are an infinite number of options and opportunities for bringing people together based upon their commonalities. Take women's groups, for example. Women in the workplace have pioneered a lot of these initiatives, such as WOW (Women on Wall Street) at New York–based Bankers Trust, which offers conferences and speakers for women in other Wall Street firms. Or Texas Instruments' WIN for SC (Women's Initiative Network for Semiconductors), which is a women's support group that also speaks to recruits. Or WITS (Women in Technology and Science) at Honeywell, which does internal mentoring for new hires.

And these initiatives do not have to be related to work. Find the common threads of interest and need in your organization and provide a forum where someone can run with it. It doesn't matter whether the basis of the group is disabilities, hobbies, or height (yes, there is even a tall person's club); "Hello, My Name is…" can add both zest and uniqueness to the daily grind. According to New York–based Catalyst, some support groups are even starting to reach out to their company's clients. These groups can do more than just help with recruitment; they can also help attract business.

Another variation on this theme is to invite an existing support group to use your company's facilities for its meetings in exchange for a reduced or free membership in the group for your own employees. This is kind of like a strategic alliance for your employees (see "1 + 1 = 3"). One of my favorite restaurants, James Street Restaurant in Pittsburgh, lets the Banjo Club meet in the restaurant every Wednesday. The club has a great place to meet and showcase its members' talents, and the restaurateur and his patrons get a free concert.

On a more serious note, this has also been done for groups on smoking cessation, weight loss, and other more personal development initiatives. But regardless of the purpose, mutual support and interest groups are a wonderful way to add value to the workplace with little or no cost or effort.

# #50 Humor Room

The first and best place I ever saw this concept used successfully was in a hospital. Not only did the hospital have a humor cart that was pushed around the wards by a clown who handed out puzzles, games, balloons, and other trinkets and trash to make people smile, it also had a humor *room* where the ambulatory patients could mingle and laugh.

This idea can work anywhere. Designate a "humor room" where people can go to let off steam and have a chuckle. It's no secret anymore that humor and laughter are healthy and rehabilitative stress relievers. Instead of just working out until they pass out, give people another outlet that makes them feel good just by being there.

Items that could be available include cartoons, gadgets, funny noses, bubbles, balloons, kazoos, comedy videos, tapes, magic tricks, games, temporary tattoos, Tinkertoys, Legos, etc. This is not a lending library (also see "Share the Wealth of Knowledge"), but a place to go to laugh. Think of it as an adult Chuck 'E' Cheez (also see "Camp MED").

## #51  Camp MED

Acxiom Corp. has a special room, similar in purpose to the humor room (see "Humor Room"), in which it has a bunch of tents set up for people to crawl into, zip up, and do whatever they need to do to get their heads back on straight. They might meditate, take a nap, read, do a puzzle, or do any number of other things in the privacy of their tent. Don't worry about it! They're pup tents, one person per tent.

Software company WRQ of Seattle, Washington, has a nap room with futons in a building with magnificent views of the mountain ranges. At Sun Microsystems in Palo Alto, California, employees can go to SunSpots, which is what Sun calls its meditation rooms. There also are SunRooms where people can play table tennis, pinball, or even trash can basketball.

Whatever you call this room or whatever you allow to be done in it, having a temporary on-site escape can be quite beneficial to both employee and employer (also see "Graffiti for Good").

## #52  It's My Party

Here's the scenario: You RSVP for a party for Saturday night. It's now Saturday afternoon, you and your significant other are hanging out, doing nothing of consequence, and one of you says, "Oh, well. I guess we'd better start getting ready for that party." Or, "I wish we hadn't agreed to go to that party." Or, "Do you think we could get out of it?"

Why in the world would you not be looking forward to a party? Because parties are usually predictable, maybe boring, or maybe even a chore. This is especially true of business functions. You have to force yourself to make conversation and act like you're interested in people you don't know or maybe don't even like, when you'd just as soon stay home and lie around in your sweats.

Here's a twist that you can use at your next party, business or otherwise, that will break the mold and make people start looking forward to your parties. In your RSVP, have the invitees complete a sentence like "People would be surprised to know that I..." with something that people wouldn't know about them. Then, type up a list of all the people's names who have RSVP'd and, across from the list of names, type the list of weird unknown things about them. As guests arrive, hand them the sheet of paper and tell them that the first person to match all the names with all the weird things will win a prize. The prize is less important than the process.

Not only is this a great way to get people out of their usual cliques, but it also creates a refreshing change of conversation from "Hi, what's your name? What do you do? Where do you live?" and all that other predictable drivel that we all hate. People actually get to know one another on a much more entertaining and significant level.

Here's another twist you can use to have some real fun. After all, it's your party, and you can do what you want! Add a few lies to the list so that there are more weird things than people and watch people try to figure out "who is the person undergoing a sex change" or "who is the person looking to have an affair." The best part is when people are down to just a couple of names, and those items are still on the list. Watch their faces.

You can also come up with a bunch of names of celebrities, politicians, cartoon characters, or any other list that fits, write them on "Hello My Name Is" tags, and, as people arrive, stick one on each person's back and require that each person find out who she or he is.

The only problem is, each person can ask each other person only three questions, and these questions must be answerable with a yes or no only. The first person to guess who he or she is can get a prize, or the last person to guess can get some type of embarrassment. Or, why not both? Once a person guesses who he or she is, that person moves the name tag to the front and can continue to take on that persona for the night, if he or she wants.

One client who wanted to celebrate diversity and was frustrated with all the challenges of political correctness decided to combine all the holidays together into one party. They got together, and each picked a holiday and brought food, decorations, and outfits to match. We had Easter eggs under the Christmas tree with Hanukah candles, green beer, and pork and sauerkraut.

Less involved ideas include just having an unusual, but participative theme, like a "creative black tie" party or a "weird hat" party. These are just a few ideas for making your parties more fun. You can come up with plenty of others.

The key is to get people out of the same old ruts and to come up with ways to change the conversation and the mingling without making it work. The last thing people want to do at a party is work. Whatever the activity, make it optional, but also make it so desirable, so much fun, and so easy that it will just happen naturally. Make your parties what they are supposed to be, i.e., something to look forward to! (Also see "Getting to Know You" for additional questions and sentences to finish.)

# #53  Let's Play Dress-Up!

There are many ways in which you can have some fun with the dress code. The obvious one is at Halloween. But, why do it when everyone else is doing it, and why restrict it to goblins and ghouls?

You can take almost any holiday (avoid the religious ones) and make it a dress-up or dress-down day. Or, you can use a special company milestone or event to have some fun with attire, like satirizing the competition, or dressing in styles from the past to celebrate the founding date for the company's anniversary. You could award a prize for the best way someone incorporates your products or services or theme into his or her wardrobe. Or, how about using current events? Our politicians provide us with endless opportunities to be weird! How about Naked Fridays? (See "Customer Appreciation Days" for some additional possibilities.)

Whatever theme or reason you choose, the point is to break the mold (see "Break the Mold") for everyone involved. Customers love weirdoes too, so let them participate whenever you can. Now that's relationship selling!

## #54 Now We're Cookin'

Anything you can do to eliminate or reduce the traditional two-class system of management and nonmanagement will be well received, at least by nonmanagement. Most smart and progressive companies have seen the benefits of the Golden Rule at work and have done away with the executive dining rooms, washrooms, preferred parking, and all the other vestiges of the Industrial Revolution. Now, let's take it a step further.

"Now We're Cookin'," in which the executive management team prepares, cooks, serves, and even cleans up after a breakfast, lunch, or dinner party, serves as a fun and symbolic equalizer. The meal can be as simple as burgers and dogs on the grill, but regardless of the ambiance, management takes orders and waits on tables. That's the whole point. Management is taking orders from nonmanagement for once.

Some organizations do this as part of another celebration, such as service awards, sales accomplishments, the annual company picnic, or some other occasion on which employees are recognized and appreciated. Or you can just do it for fun. Sometimes these gestures have more impact if they are done for no special reason at all, except to let people know that you care. Actions speak louder than words, especially in the workplace.

# #55   Oh, Baby!

This idea is real simple. Get people to bring in a picture from their early childhood, number the pictures, and post them where people can look at them, laugh, and guess who they are. This can also be incorporated into a contest, or even a fundraiser for a children's benefit.

Make it a 50-50 contest. For a buck, you can enter your guesses; whoever guesses the most right gets half the pot, with the other half going to a children's benefit of the winner's choice. Or, you may have some preselected and approved charities from which the winner can choose.

Another variation is to have award categories, like the ugliest baby, the cutest baby, the weirdest setting or picture, or any other fun, weird categories you choose. Then award trophies or gag prizes for the various category winners.

# #56   Show 'n' Tell

"Show 'n' Tell" is about sharing stuff. Have people bring in their personal treasures for display. Set up tables in your cafeteria or conference room or, if enough people bring things in, get a meeting room or ballroom at a local hotel for the show. Give the show a unique and fun name, like "Trash and Treasures," "Treasure Island," or "I'll Show You Mine," or, of course, "Show 'n' Tell!"

Ask people to bring in something that is special to them. It could be a piece of art, a souvenir from a far-away place, an heirloom, or any other item that they feel either is unique or has an interesting story to accompany it. Some of the best treasures are those from people's early childhood, such as old toys, stuffed animals, comic books, trophies, model cars, trains, baseball cards, or baby dolls.

Be sure to ask people to explain why the particular item is special to them. In fact, ask them to type up a one-sheet description of what the treasure is and why it is special. Compile the sheets as a program for the show and then have each participant display this description with the show 'n' tell item so that others can appreciate it without the participant's having to explain it over and over or having to stand there for the whole show—unless of course, that's what you want participants to do. You could even have the items' owners remain anonymous and turn this into a contest to guess who belongs to what.

Another fun variation on this theme is an employee "Pet Show." You can have various awards for things like the *most unusual, ugliest, cutest, meanest, stinkiest, funniest,* or any other categories that might fit the bill. A note of caution: Be sure you hold this in a place without carpeting, and check your liability insurance beforehand.

# #57 Talent Show

When you meet someone for the first time and that person asks the standard question, "What do you do?" do you respond with what you do at work? I'm an accountant. I'm an engineer. I'm in sales. Most people do. Next time, say "I fish!" or "I sing!" or "I garden!" The fun part is to watch their reaction. Now, that's weird!

The point here is that the people in your organization are not just job titles. They are usually multitalented or have multiple interests. Find out what these talents and interests are and who has them by organizing a talent show. A lot of techies, for example, are very much into music and extreme sports. Many are in garage bands or other extracurricular activities as participants, not just observers (see "Rock Me, Baby!"). In fact, the CEO of Third Federal Savings & Loan in Cleveland, Ohio, is the lead vocalist in a "company" rock band. Many people who have to use their left brain all day doing logical, analytical activities will find right-brained diversions, like acting, singing, or painting, in their nonwork life, and vice versa (see "Get a Life").

Before you announce such a talent show, send out an inquiry or survey to find out what other talents, interests, and diversions your people have (see "Brainpower Inventory"), and then ask if they would be willing and interested in sharing these talents with others.

The actual program can be done at lunchtime, or it can be a separate, dedicated, special event. If it is done at lunchtime, you can have one performance a day for a long time. If it is summertime, or if you are one of those fortunate ones who live in year-round summer, make it an outside concert or show. You might even get some free publicity in the local media.

## #58 That's Entertainment

Find a local theater company, performing arts school, or other "off-Broadway" or amateur talent group to come to your organization to do a mini-show. This is particularly easy to do if the performers are trying to market a current or upcoming show, because they will jump at the chance to give a preview version or mini-show as a teaser promotion. If you have a comedy club in town, find out who is playing and invite them in for a sample show. It's free advertising of the best kind. (Be sure to check out their brand of entertainment beforehand to avoid the embarrassment of profanity or other material that is inappropriate in the workplace.)

Even if you have to pay for this, most local performers, or even traveling performers who happen to be in town, are quite reasonable in their rates. In fact, many will do it for free in order to bolster box office sales. There are also many improvisation groups that not only are entertaining, but can also tailor the show to your audience and your theme (also see "Training Theater").

Other options include jugglers, musicians, magicians, mimes, and even dancers and gymnasts. Don't call the local union or a talent agency unless you want to pay through the nose. Why do you think they're called "starving artists"? They'll work for food! (Just kidding. Lighten up!)

## #59 Work Smells

What does it smell like to work at your company? Why should you care? Well, unless you want to continue to be generic in every regard, think about changing your environment in a sensory way. As we all know, first impressions are powerful, and smell is one of the easiest, yet most innovative and powerful ways of making a subtle, yet very effective statement.

I have seen this concept implemented most effectively in the health care field because every doctor's office and every hospital smells alike. You could be blind and know that you are in a medical office. Wouldn't it be a pleasant surprise to walk into a hospital or a doctor's or dentist's office and smell potpourri instead of antiseptic? Espresso instead of sterilizer? Popcorn instead of plastic? You can become as innovative as you want to in this one, and it costs next to nothing, particularly compared to the effect you will generate.

The main idea is to positively surprise people the second they walk in the door. Their senses are directly connected to their moods, and their first impressions establish how they are going to react to the rest of their experience with your organization (also see "Break the Mold").

## #60 You Can Call Me Ray!

Some of you may be too young to remember the beer commercial where the guy says, "You can call me Ray, or you can call me Jay...," but in any event, the essence of this idea is to let people create their own unique identities at work.

This idea is an extension of the "Lose the Legalese" idea. More and more fun and progressive organizations are allowing people more latitude in the titles they adopt. Lighten up! In fact, the word employee is even becoming passé. People are now associates or team members or partners, or even owners.

At Orlando Regional Healthcare, people are *careholders*. At places like Guidant, Acxiom, or Granite Rock, they are *employee-owners* or *job-owners*. Some even incorporate the company name into their titles. For example, at American Management Systems, they are AMSers; at Microstrategy, they are Microstrategists; at Scitor, they are Scitorians; at Trilogy, they are Trilogians.

Some new titles have just evolved on their own out of pure necessity, like CIO (chief information officer), but others have been created with nothing but fun and weirdness in mind. Some that I have seen include Duke of Cool, ISO Queen, Guru of Fun, VP of People, Information Highwayman, Technology evangelist, and even Troublemaker. Kyle Shannon of Agency.com Ltd. (an Internet professional services firm in New York) went from the already creative title of Chief Creative Officer to C3PO, which is to represent his role as Chief People, Progress, and Potential Officer (he manages internal employee relations and external recruiting).

Tom Peters suggests that all CEOs worth their salary should change their title to CDO (chief destruction officer) because to be true agents of change, they must be ready, willing, and able to blow it all up and start over again.

At Scitor, a project management consultancy in Sunnyvale, California, people pick their own title. Even if you need to keep traditional titles for the purposes of the outside world or to fill in the blanks on your anal-retentive organization chart, you can still allow people to have some fun with their "working titles." The world will not end. And don't forget to provide people with business cards, name tents, and other workplace title paraphernalia (see "Cards for Everyone!"). (For many more examples of job titles of the future, go to www.fastcompany.com/online/resources/jobtitle.html.)

# #61 You're a Winner!

Contests are one of the best ways to get people excited and involved. In their best form, they also have a purpose. For example, you might ask people to submit their ideas for improvements, or for a conference theme, or to name the company newsletter. Whatever the purpose, be sure that the more involved a person gets, the more chances he or she has to win. It's pay for performance wrapped in fun. Each entry earns another ticket into the sweepstakes, and at a certain point in time (it could be a one-time contest or a recurring one, such as quarterly or monthly) all entries are closed and a winner or winners are drawn.

As in any such effort, the manner in which the winner is selected and announced is as important as the contest itself. Be sure to make it an event (maybe a lunch or at some other all-employee gathering); if that's not possible, at least showcase the winner(s) in some very fun, visible way. You want nonparticipants to feel that they have missed out on something in order to increase the likelihood of their participation in future contests.

The key objectives are employee involvement and enthusiasm. Another advantage to contests is that they can be kept fresh without a lot of effort. You can change the theme or thrust as often as you like, which keeps the contest (and your employees) from becoming stale. It could be a reward for cross-selling, upselling, referral of business or recruits, safety records, attendance records, product knowledge, or anything of high importance that is worth emphasizing at the moment.

You can also change the reward. In fact, you should. The more variety in the rewards, the more relevant to individuals and the more desirable they become. Ideally, winners should be able to choose their own award (see "Get the Point[s]"). In any event, if there is a single type of award, be sure that it has universal appeal (like time off, money, etc.).

## #62 You're Kidding!

We're all familiar with the "take your daughter to work day" concept, which in some places became the "take your kid to work day" when the ironically sexist nature of the day imploded upon itself.

Forget about whether your kid is a boy or a girl, or even if it's your kid! Just open your doors to children once a year for all kinds of reasons, beyond just "look what Daddy or Mommy does all day when he or she is not being a parent."

Whether you do it purely for public relations or to allow your employees to share their work lives with their dependents, the experience is a win-win. Organize the day to include lunch with the CEO, or to see the "fun" parts of the company (which may not be considered fun by stiff old adults), like where the trucks come in and out (shipping and receiving) or where all the scrap ends up. Don't assume that just because you are enthralled by watching tech service answer all those phones all day, kids give a darn about it. Put yourself into a kid's perspective and mindset. That alone may be worth the exercise!

Be sure to have ice cream, entertainment, activities, contests, banners, and all kinds of kid-friendly ambiance available. Include your employees in the planning and implementation—it is, after all, for their kids! And don't forget the souvenir trinkets and trash with your logo on it (also see "Trinkets and Trash").

Finally, if the CEO or some other VIP is going to address the group, be sure to have someone review the script or speech ahead of time. I have seen little eyes glaze over quite rapidly when some old guy starts talking about market share or total quality improvement or some other corporate gobbledygook. Use the third grader test. That is, have an eight-year-old read the speech and circle any words she or he doesn't understand, then change those words. Keep it short; keep it simple; keep it fun(ny).

Having curious, innocent little minds and bodies running around once in a while invigorates the entire workplace and introduces your potential future workforce to your organization through a fun and positive experience. Another win-win!

# WeIRD IDeAS FOR PeRKS, PAY, AND PATS ON THE BAcK

## aka RECOGNITION & INCENTIVES

*Some of the ideas in this book apply equally to employee recognition and retention. After all, lack of suitable recognition and rewards is cited as a leading cause of employee dissatisfaction and turnover, so if you can make some strides in recognition, you will automatically improve your chances of keeping good people.*

*It has been said several times in this book that compensation is not the only variable in successful employee recruitment, retention, and motivation. If there is one employee need that does seem to be universal, however, it is to be recognized for a job well done, or even for something totally unrelated to one's direct output, like maybe a birthday.*

*I remember seeing a sign in someone's cubicle that said, "Why is it that no one notices what I do around here, until I stop doing it?" Let's start noticing!*

## #63 Ambassadors, Advocates, and Apostles

Once that you have turned everyone you know into a recruiter for your company (see "Bird Dog Biscuits"), you need to make everyone a sales rep as well. Create ways for your employees, your vendors, your suppliers, and even your current customers to refer new business to you by giving them business referral cards that they can put their names on when they solicit new business. Make them "Ambassadors, Advocates, and Apostles" (AAA). Put business referral cards or coupons in or on your product packaging, send out a special promotion to your vendors, suppliers, customers, and employees, or come up with your own way of communicating the "share the wealth" idea. Just as in "Bird Dog Biscuits," you shouldn't limit who is "eligible" to add customers. Any source is a good source if it results in new business.

You do not have to pay in cash (although no one will complain if you do), but the more referral cards that come back to the company, the more chances the person making the referrals should have to win great prizes (trips, getaway weekends, points toward bigger and bigger awards, etc.). (This is discussed further in "Get the Point[s].") Repeat behavior should be worth more than one-time behavior.

I saw this idea work very well in the restaurant business when the owner gave employees promotional discount coupons on which the employee's name or number could be imprinted or written in. When a customer redeemed a coupon, it went into a hopper, and once a month during a staff meeting, a winner was pulled. This is a particularly effective method because people are rewarded only for coupons that have been redeemed, which is the whole point of a promotional coupon.

Remember, always try to present rewards and recognition in public forums. This has much more impact for the recipient, it adds an element of excitement, and it also reminds those who are slow to participate that they are missing out on something good, thus improving the odds for increased future participation. Just remember the adage: "Punish privately; praise publicly."

## #64 Wall of Fame

A key building block of organizational success is showing off your successes to the world. Many employees are never aware of what is going right, who is doing well, or even why or whether they should feel proud. Even if you take advantage of opportunities to reward or recognize accomplishments as they occur, it is equally as important to archive and showcase these accomplishments on an ongoing basis. Think of it as a trophy case.

And don't limit your "Wall of Fame" to major product or service breakthroughs (that might produce a tiny trophy case for a while). Include letters of commendation and awards from outside the organization, both individual and organizational, and take advantage of any opportunity you can to make your people feel that they are in the company of winners. In fact, peer recognition awards are every bit as appropriate for the "Wall of Fame" as any other type of recognition (also see "Peer Pats").

Most of all, be sure your "Wall of Fame" is visible to outsiders, such as customers, vendors, and candidates. Locate it in the lobby or in some other "first impression" location. And please keep it current and keep it clean! Nothing is more depressing or contradictory or sends a more mixed message than a display of moldy and tarnished old trophies in a showcase layered in dust. The "Wall of Fame" can be a powerful PR tool as well as a motivational one.

# #65 One-Minute Parades

This is a take-off on the embarrassing practice in some restaurants of singing "Happy Birthday" around your table in front of a bunch of total strangers. Although you could do it on birthdays, you can adapt this idea to the workplace by doing it for anyone who has won an award, achieved a milestone, finished a big project, or attained any other incremental goal.

But rather than just standing around a cubicle singing, have a parade! Get people marching around the office with whatever personal "floats" they can create, hats, noisemakers, and any other festive garb they can come up with. It only needs to last a minute. In fact, anything longer than that is awkward, unnecessary, and overkill. Just have someone send out a confidential notice that there will be a one-minute parade and give the who, the when, the where, and especially the why so that people can prepare.

There is usually a lot of pent-up creative energy waiting to be set free in high-performance and/or high-stress workplaces. "One-Minute Parades" are a simple, fun, and effective way to involve everyone in recognizing people on the spot, for anything you want.

# #66 Name That Room

Another way of recognizing special people, even temporarily, is to name things after them, preferably while they are still alive. You can use the cafeteria, hallways, or meeting rooms. (Even restrooms could be used in jest—it could be called "John's John" or "Sally's Stall" or something equally irreverent.) But, just as Cape Kennedy became Cape Canaveral again, nothing has to be permanent. In this case, it's probably better that it isn't, to allow more people to be similarly honored.

Another way to use this idea is to "Name That Room" to honor your major accounts/customers by recognizing their contribution to your organization's success. Avoid using your restrooms for them! Be sure to have a dedication ceremony with key decision makers and stakeholders present. It costs nothing and gains everything. It also serves as a reminder to your employees to honor thy customer every day.

Another variation is to just name every room something. MECC (formerly Minnesota Educational Computing Corporation) made fun of itself by realizing that one of its conference rooms was really small and dubbed it the "Notalotaroom." (Figure it out?) One of MECC's key products was an educational software program called Munchers, so the cafeteria was named "Muncher Hall." In keeping with the education theme, the company also had "Home Room," one of the conference rooms was called the "Think Tank," and various other parts of the campus had relevant, but fun names.

Here's one you'll really love. The conference rooms at the Santa Clara, California, offices of Web company Yahoo! have names like Coherent, Disposed, Consistent, and Definitely. Think about it. Have you figured it out? If someone asks, "Where's John?" you can say, "Oh, he's in Coherent" or "He's in Disposed" or "He's in Consistent."

Again, you can combine ideas by having a "Name That Room" contest for common areas and rooms (lobbies, conference rooms, cafeterias, hallways) and awarding prizes for most creative, most relevant, etc. Have fun with it!

# #67 Public Résumés

Although you may not want to go into as much depth and detail as the 4 E's (see "Getting to Know You"), the idea of public résumés is to tell the world who your people are. The best example I have seen of this was in an automobile dealer's service department. Above each technician's bay (no, they are not called mechanics any more) was a large, hanging placard with the technician's name, years of experience, certifications, specialties, awards, and even hobbies and interests. What used to be called stalls or bays were now called the technician's offices.

Not surprisingly, knowing something about the people who were working on their cars made the customers feel better. It also gave the technicians both pride and ownership in their workspace, resulting in improved housekeeping and maintenance. It also gave those technicians who had not earned as many awards or certifications as others an incentive to start thinking more about their personal development.

Like most of the ideas in this book, public résumés could be incorporated into almost any workplace. Rather than just putting a nameplate on somebody's door or cubicle wall, why not create a summary sheet describing *the person* for others to see. You will be surprised how little your own people know about one another until you do something like this. (Also see "Brainpower Inventory.")

A photograph of the employee may also be a nice touch, particularly for visitors and for new employees who do not know everyone yet. One company has a caricature (a cartoon drawing with exaggerated features, like is done at festivals and fairs) drawn for every employee and has it framed and hung outside the employee's office or cubicle. Same purpose, but more fun.

You may want this to be voluntary and the information included to be at the option and discretion of the individual, but once the public résumés and/or photos or caricatures are accepted as a common practice, people will generally participate fully and positively. Even though some people *act* embarrassed about touting their strengths or interests, everyone eventually likes to have the opportunity to be known in a positive way, and this makes it politically correct to do so.

## #68 No Parking

Many companies use a reserved parking spot near the entrance for the "employee of the month," but why restrict this to one program? It could be an add-on perk for many of the other ideas in this book. Whoever gets the most points in a quarter (see "Get the Point[s]") could get a reserved parking spot for a month. Whoever wins the "Name That Room" contest could get a spot. Just look at all the ideas in this book and think about how a prize parking spot might be an appropriate reward. Be sure you put the person's name on the spot so that the whole world can see it, and so that the employee can see it every day when coming and going.

On a related note, do not have permanent reserved spots for executives and managers. This is a highly outdated concept and a real downer for everyone else, particularly if everyone else arrives for work before the privileged few do. Parking should be first come, first get, period. It's also rather refreshing to see the CEO running across the parking lot dodging the raindrops.

It may sound petty, but these "two-class systems," no matter how well-intentioned, can damage the morale of any organization, particularly if the organization has the gall to be preaching teamwork and the "one big happy family" theme at the same time.

This equality thing extends to the executive washroom, the executive dining room, and most of the other segregated executive amenities. Can you believe that a *Fortune 100* company I used to work for even had a separate executive elevator? I guess they were afraid of catching those low-class cooties all the rest of us had.

At Intel, the giant chipmaker in Santa Clara, California, not only are there no reserved parking spaces, but everyone, including the CEO, works in a cubicle. As this book keeps emphasizing, *actions speak louder than words!*

## #69 I'll Scratch Yours

If it's truly better to give than to receive, this one's a winner. Give everyone in the company a voucher, a ticket, a certificate, or some other redeemable coupon that is worthless until it is given away. The only way it can have value is by being endorsed by someone else, along with the reason for giving it to him or her.

The thinking behind this is to begin the concept of 360-degree recognition and rewards, to include everyone across the board, and to make people think about whom they really appreciate and why. So if you are a really helpful, valued person, you may get a whole bunch of these vouchers; if not, all you can do is give one away.

The reason I call it "I'll Scratch Yours" is because the first time I saw this done, the company used those scratch-off tickets with the gray crud that had to be removed to see what you won. Although this is not necessary, it did add another fun dimension to the process, made the value of the reward random (and thus fair), and also allowed a few larger prizes to be included while minimizing the risk of sour grapes on the part of those who didn't win them.

You could always combine this idea with "Get the Point(s)" and make the coupons worth a certain number of points—the more you are able to accumulate, the more you can get for them. Or, you could allow people to combine them departmentally for something even bigger, like a catered lunch or party, a new piece of equipment for the lunchroom, or some other group benefit.

To get the most bang for your buck, publish the various reasons that were written on the vouchers so that people can see the types of behaviors that are valued, and have a special award ceremony for the person or department that hauled in the most.

# #70 Peer Pats

There's a lot of talk about recognition and rewards, but most people seem to think that these must come from above, i.e., from the boss. However, some of the most valued recognition comes from our peers, since they probably see and know what we do better than most others.

Even though people ought to thank and acknowledge one another without a formal process to make it happen, some people are uncomfortable with it or just don't know how to do it. The answer is to create a way for people to pat each other on the back in a simple, politically correct and effective manner.

In one approach that I have seen, a simple gold coin, similar in appearance to an Olympic gold medal, is passed on to someone at a monthly meeting of all employees. Whoever was awarded the coin (or coins) at the prior meeting is responsible for identifying someone at the next meeting to pass it on to, along with a specific reason for doing so, which is articulated in front of the group when the coin is passed on.

You need not restrict this to one coin. You could have a series of coins that are used for this purpose. The value is not in the coin(s) but in the activity of recognizing someone and saying why, and eventually involving as many people as possible in the process.

Another variation, which can be used for departments or individuals, is to have a trophy that travels throughout the organization, based upon whatever criteria you like. Think of it as being like the National Hockey League's Stanley Cup, which no one owns, but everyone wants. You can't keep it unless you continue to be the best. It is cherished, but never permanent. This also saves on the cost of trophies. You need only one!

Finally, you might want to do what Ukrop's Super Markets in Richmond, Virginia, does. It gives managers a "Thank-You Kit" with thank-you notes and money to dole out for movie tickets, flowers, or any number of things. What you put in your kit is up to you. It's pretty sad that we have to teach people how to give praise and have to give them tools and templates, but if that's what it takes to make it happen, it's better than no praise at all.

## #71 Bribe the Bride (or Groom, or Domestic Partner)

No, this is not some sexist idea. The reason I call it "Bribe the Bride" is because the first time I ever saw this done was for a newlywed male employee who had to work inordinately long hours right after his honeymoon, thus neglecting his new bride. It can go either way.

Do you have employees who put in long hours or have to be away from home for extended periods, particularly during crunch times? If so, don't just thank the employee who has been living at work. Thank her or his mate, too. A great way to get maximum mileage out of recognition is to send your employee's husband, wife, or partner a gift of flowers, candy, cookies, balloons, or some other fun token of your appreciation. And don't tell your employee you are doing it. Make it a surprise for him or her, too!

Attach a note that reads something like, "Thank you for sharing Mary with us these past few weeks (months) during Project X. We realize that this has been as much of a sacrifice for you and your family as it has for her. Please accept this gift as a token of our appreciation." This acknowledges the mate as part of the bigger team.

If the budget allows, the best gift is one that the couple can enjoy together, like dinner for two at their favorite restaurant or a getaway weekend at a nice hotel, resort, or spa. And please, don't require your employee to use his or her vacation or other paid time off for this. This is a gift! If the effort is worth rewarding, don't shoot yourself in the foot by making the employee subsidize it or make further sacrifices in order to use it. You don't reward a past sacrifice by asking for another.

Extending this idea to the whole family, there are even those who give gifts to the children of employees who have sacrificed their family time for the company. They might get a video game, a toy, a day at an amusement park, or some other fun gift. If you want to see a powerful retention tool, try telling your kids that you are changing jobs when they have been getting great stuff from your current employer!

## #72 Cooperation Compensation

If you like the idea of breaking down organizational barriers (see "Silo Destruction") and would like to add a bomb to it to make it happen, try "Cooperation Compensation." Basic organizational behavior theory says, "That which is observed, measured, and rewarded gets done." This is an idea that will guarantee improved "internal" customer service.

I first learned of this idea from Wilson Harrell, a consultant to entrepreneurs and a regular contributor to the former *Success* magazine. In his consulting business, departments graded each other's performance once a month and bonuses were issued based upon the results.

Each month, each department head met face to face with each of the others and listed what he or she expected. Harrell called these lists "Care-Abouts." After each meeting, both department heads signed off on their commitment to perform the services on the list. And, every month, every department graded the others on a scale of 1 to 10. The grades were then averaged and published for the whole company to see. As Harrell says, "Suddenly, there's no place to hide. A department either met its commitments or it didn't, and the whole company knows it."

The effect was dramatic. When a department head got a low grade from another, it got his or her attention, in part because he or she knew that it got the CEO's attention. Suddenly, there was an intense desire among the heads to work things out. Instead of running to the CEO for their usual politicking session, they just quietly solved problems. Harrell says that he saw executives who had never gotten along suddenly cozying up. That alone saved the CEO a lot of time. He could also run down the list of departmental grades once a month and quickly see where the problems were.

A percentage of everyone's salary was affected by his or her department's grade. If a department got a 10 from all the others, all its employees got the maximum. If the average was 7 or less, the employees got no bonus that month. To quote Harrell, "I don't need to tell you that the words *cooperation* and *coordination* take on new meaning. People use their initiative to benefit themselves and the company."

## #73 Get the Point(s)

As you have seen, most of the ideas in this book can be tailored and tweaked almost limitlessly, and this one truly exemplifies that quality. The behavioral objective behind allowing people to "earn" points, and accumulate and save them, is to encourage repeat behavior, which ultimately leads to permanent changes in habits. Rewarding a behavior once is nice, but increasing the rewards for repeat behavior is even better.

For example, let's say you wanted people to start looking for ways to improve operations, cut costs, or some other initiative. You might reward each good idea that is adopted and implemented with a certificate worth a certain number of points. The key words here are *adopted* and *implemented*. Do not pay for an idea that has no chance of being used or having its value realized.

Another way to enhance the value of "Get the Point(s)" and to ensure that good ideas are implemented is to set up a separate reward schedule for those who are responsible for implementation. They can earn rewards for timely approval of ideas (thus reducing the tendency to "just say no"), for setting their own deadlines for implementation, and ultimately for meeting those deadlines. Following through on this logic, you might even set up a measuring and monitoring reward to ensure that the value of the idea is truly realized.

Using blocks of at least 1,000 points each tends to work well, even if 1,000 points is only worth a dollar or maybe ten dollars. When designing the "redemption schedule" for points, make sure the employees are better off if they save their points and accumulate even more of them for even better rewards. Maybe 1,000 points is worth a free lunch, but 5,000 points is worth a half day of indulgence at a spa! Backload the point schedule to make the higher point values disproportionately more valuable, thus rewarding repeat behavior more than one-time behavior. Remember, your ultimate objective is to change behavior permanently.

Another key is to provide a large enough variety of awards (in type and value) that there will be something that appeals to everyone, and that some awards will be valuable enough to encourage repeat behavior, which will ultimately create permanent changes in behavior. Make new habits worthwhile!

Have you noticed that I use the word *earn* rather than *win?* This may seem trivial, but there is a rather profound distinction. This is not a lottery or a sweepstakes. It is something that people must earn through their efforts. This also advances the cause of pay for performance, not pay for just being there.

One of the more creative and original programs I have seen was at Wells Fargo in California, which had 101 awards, all listed on one page. They were quite diverse, creative, and sometimes even humorous. Here are a few of them:

Grooming for your pet for a year

Once-a-month house cleaning for six months

A year's worth of pantyhose

$1,000 worth of eldercare or daycare

A star named after you

An all-expense-paid trip to the annual shareholders meeting with an introduction

A two-hour body massage on April 15

Twenty hours of music or sports lessons for you or your kid

A hot air balloon ride

A makeover

An easy way to remember the greater goal in "Get the Point(s)" is to think of the acronym IBM (for incremental behavior modification). I have seen companies implement formal programs to solicit new ideas in which they actually had rewards just for showing up for the launch announcement meeting. One of the top companies that designs these programs is Maritz, Inc., of Fenton, Missouri.

The reward for showing up was a logo pen, because the next incremental behavior the company was looking for was signing up to participate in the program (the employees already have the pen!). Then there would be a slightly greater reward for signing up (maybe a coffee mug, duffel bag, or other logo item). Next, there would be an incrementally greater reward for submitting their first idea (even a bad one) just to recognize the effort, followed by greater and greater rewards for submitting *good* ideas that can be implemented (which is where the point system comes in). Little by little the company was moving the employees toward high performance in painless, incremental steps, i.e., IBM. Show up, sign up, put up.

Another advantage to using a cumulative point system is that you can post names or teams and their respective point standings in a public place, which not only recognizes their efforts even further, but also generates some healthy peer envy, particularly among the nonparticipants, and encourages some fun competition among the current leaders. If this is done correctly, at some point even the doubters and stragglers will usually start to get on board. And if some of them do not, this is a great way to identify or confirm your hopeless cases.

Also, when your winners order their awards, be sure they are shipped to your company to your attention, so you can "present" them in public. It's even more fun if you can accumulate a bunch of prizes in a room somewhere to create a little excitement and anticipation. Presenting the awards at lunchtime or in some other public forum is another way of adding impetus to the stragglers' jumping on board before it is too late.

Finally, I recommend that you change the theme as often as your organizational needs dictate. For six months you might reward cross-selling or upselling. The following six months you might reward safety or quality. The sky's the limit! Keep it fresh and exciting! Oh, and by the way, don't forget to give the program a weird name. And, put that name on all the logo rewards too.

## #74 Gimme a Break!

Although the basic product/service discount idea is not a new one, there are a few new twists that you can use. First of all, what if your product or service is of no interest or value to your employees? For example, if you sell high-end industrial supplies or equipment, there aren't too many individuals who have the need, the interest, or the budget to buy a hydraulic crane.

So, why not set up a bartering arrangement with a company that *does* buy your products or services to offer *your* employees a discount on *its* products or services. It is not uncommon for companies to offer supplier or vendor discounts, so there is no reason that this benefit could not be reversed to extend discounts to the employees of *their* suppliers and vendors. Ideally, the arrangement would go both ways, which is the perfect way to introduce the idea. But even if it cannot, there is no reason not to suggest an arrangement for your employees to become customers of your customers too.

Another extension of this benefit is to offer the benefit to the families of your employees. How you define *family* is entirely up to you. If you want to be stingy, you can limit it to just the immediate family (spouse and kids), but you can also define a more extended family, like anyone living in the household, or even publish a list of relatives who qualify. Even if your employees don't have a need for or an interest in your products or services, they may have relatives who do.

For companies that do have products or services that might appeal to employees and their families, it is a little easier. Employees at Ben & Jerry's get three pints of ice cream per day. That's nice, but would you believe that the pharmaceutical giant Pfizer gives its employees free drugs, including Viagra? I'll bet that's a happy workplace! If that isn't enough, you can go to work at Eli Lilly and get the same free drug benefit, but this time it includes Prozac. Employees of the Four Seasons hotel chain and their families can book rooms for free. All employees at America-Online get two free AOL accounts, one for themselves and one for a friend. Can you see the underlying strategy in this? Lucas Digital (of George Lucas fame) has weekly first-run movie screenings for employees.

You can let your imagination run wild with what employees at other companies might be able to get, but take a look at whether your company might be able to offer some "value" to your people, either directly or indirectly.

# #75 Show Me the Money NOW!

We are all aware of the traditional bonus plans that have been available in many companies in the past. We also know that they are usually complex or reserved only for higher-ups and/or tend to lack a short-term, day-to-day correlation with behavior; i.e., they are not pay for performance, and they are not cost-effective.

Organizational behavior theory tells us that humans aren't really much different from the pets they own when it comes to behavior modification. This is particularly true for the concept of immediacy. The more closely the reward is linked to the behavior, in both time and value, the more likely it is that the behavior will be repeated.

If Fido rolls over upon command, you don't wait until next Tuesday to give him a cookie. If you do, he will connect the reward to whatever his most recent behavior was, which may have been chewing up your shoes. The same thing goes for employees. If I do something right, let me know right away and let me feel good about it right away. Good boy! Here's a cookie!

Here's a case in point: I had a client whose business used minimum-wage, high school–age front-line service employees. Can you think of a more challenging combination of variables? You may not be surprised to hear that this client had an occasional absenteeism problem. He realized that his employees really did not place much value on their jobs or fear being fired, because they could just walk down the street and start work for someone else the next day at the same wage. Sound familiar?

His first inclination was to improve the pay scale in hopes that his employees would think twice about missing work because they wouldn't want to lose this better-paying job. The problem was that the most he could afford to increase their pay, and still be competitive, was about 50 cents an hour. For a full-time employee, this amounted to a mere $4 per day extra—not enough to win the battle between sleeping in and going to work on time.

However, using the principles of immediacy and value, that same 50 cents per hour translates into $86 when multiplied times 172 working hours in a month. So, instead of the reward and punishment being structured in increments of $4 (and being somewhat invisible when it was lumped into the regular paycheck), he rewarded each *month* of perfect attendance with a whopping $86 bonus check at the end of the month! For a minimum-wage employee, this is a chunk of change that cannot be ignored. Now, when the alarm clock rings and Joe Employee is debating between playing Frisbee in the park or working for a living, the job looks like the better choice.

This reward is short-term, attainable, visible, and valuable. And, if the employee does have to miss a day, he or she isn't out of the game next month. In fact, this employer could have probably gotten away with paying less than 50 cents per hour without losing the impact of this technique because of the multiplier effect of accumulating the increase over 172 hours. The other advantage to this approach is that the employee who does not respond to this incentive costs the employer nothing extra. In the first scenario, all the employees got 50 cents per hour more *whenever* they were there! Again, this is true pay for performance.

Just as a footnote, after a few months this employer had a new problem because of this program. Because people wanted their bonus so badly, some were coming to work when they were in no condition to work. In other words, they would crawl into work sick so that they wouldn't lose their bonus. Nice problem! To reward the effort, the owner would acknowledge their dedication, send them home and give them some type of bonus anyway.

Wouldn't you rather have the problem of having to send home people who were sick than the problem of trying to drag them out of bed when they are perfectly well? You can be the good guy while changing their work habits at the same time.

Another strength of this "simple bonus" concept is that the focus can be changed frequently, keeping the program fresh and current.

It can be applied and modified to reinforce many different types of workplace behaviors, such as safety, punctuality, or appearance. You decide, but just be sure to "show them the money *now!*"

## #76 What Are My Options?

In their quest to get and keep rare talent, more and more companies that started offering company stock options have now found themselves in a sticky dilemma. First, there are only so many options to go around; second, not everyone deserves them; and third, their value has proved to be quite volatile. Unfortunately, in the world of techies with rare talent, they also started to become an expectation.

Sun Microsystems was one of the first technology companies to try out a new "options model" rather than giving out the traditional piece of the company action. Rather than give everyone options in the company, it identified projects that were considered critical to the company's future, then created "shares" in those projects, complete with documents resembling stock certificates, and distributed them to engineers working on relevant project teams.

At the end of a fixed time period, usually three to five years, the shares are turned into cash based upon the profits that the project(s) generate. This concept puts a premium on timely performance, because the longer a product is on the market, rather than in the lab, the greater the profit potential.

The program also matches rewards to results. If a team of engineers delivers a great product, the members will win big even if the company as a whole had a disappointing year. Engineers who participate in the program can end up making a lot of money, but only if they stick around. If they leave, they lose, so not only is this a great pay for performance idea, but it also serves as a more effective retention strategy, particularly in an environment where traditional stock options may have plummeted.

# WeIRD IDeAS FOR EDuCATInG ToDAY'S TALeNT

## aka TRAINING & DEVELOPMENT

*The only thing worse than training people and having them leave is not training them and having them stay! Why is training important? Traditionally, most companies have looked at training as a way to improve job skills. That's fine, but what then? Is training just for teaching people how to do their job faster or better? I don't think so. And neither do all the high-performance workers out there who can do their job just fine, and can do it anywhere. These are whole-brained people with a need to use their whole brain eventually, somewhere.*

*The ideas in this section can be used for the traditional job skill type of training, but there is a larger behavior modification objective, as well. After all, what is the point of training people to become the best at what they do if they end up leaving to do it for someone else? Maybe even a competitor?*

*Many of the ideas in this section could have just as easily been placed in the retention section, because training (both job-related and non-job-related) is also a key component in keeping your best people.*

# #77 Do Your Workwork!

Orientation is the first training your new employees receive in their new environment. I am always amazed at how companies fail to capitalize on the impact they could have during this period. When I ask a group of company representatives for a show of hands on whether they have an orientation program, I almost always get less than 100 percent response. My reply is that every company has a new employee orientation program, whether the company knows it or not.

Somehow, your new employees "learn the lessons" from someone. Unfortunately, if this is not orchestrated by you, they may be learning the inside scoop from one of your worst employees. "Don't worry about coming in on time on Wednesdays because the boss always has an outside meeting that day." "You can shortcut this form/procedure because it is only audited once a year." Sound familiar? Either way, you are paying for an orientation, so why not have it work to your advantage?

If it's called homework when you do it at home, it must be workwork if you do it at work, right? Here's a fun twist on new employee orientations. Rather than structure a day here and an hour there talking with people who just tell the new employee what they "think" she or he should know (and boring the hell out of her or him), create a workbook that the new hire completes by answering questions and filling in blanks. MEMC Electronic Materials in St. Peters, Missouri (one of the world's largest producers of silicon wafers), assigns "The Paper." New employees spend four weeks doing the necessary research to write a complete report on all the performance parameters of a step of the manufacturing process. Part

of the reason for this is that this industry is one of the most techni-
cally demanding industries for new recruits to understand.

New engineers at MEMC spend two days learning the company
history and operations, then receive a workbook with questions on
every aspect of the company, including their benefits package. They
have three months to answer hundreds of such questions. And the
only way this can be done is to talk to people all over the company
(also see "Silo Destruction").

One of the keys is that you must be willing to give the new
employee a certain amount of time to visit whatever people and
departments might have answers in areas like the company history,
operations, manufacturing trivia, product or service applications,
employee benefits, or whatever else that would make up a good,
rounded base of knowledge and expedite his or her assimilation to
the culture of the company. This is a compressed, programmed net-
working activity designed to get new employees to go outside their
department and get to know the people and the company in a more
interactive and entertaining way.

You can also have a prize for completing the exercise, like some
type of logo wear or some other symbol of "belonging" to the organization. Orientation is not just for the purpose of giving and getting
information; it is also a way of instilling values and making a powerful and positive first impression.

# #78 Collect the Dots

This concept was born in an upscale fast-food franchise
where young, minimum-wage workers were expected to
pay attention to detail, particularly in the areas of restaurant hygiene
and cleanliness. Getting them to do this was not an easy task.

The "normal" approach to this would be to train and monitor
for proper behaviors. That works fine as long as you are there to
watch. Remember, this is not career employment for most of these
people. So, in order to drive the point home and to make it fun,
the owner/manager of this particular restaurant chain went out

and bought a box of colored sticky dots and stuck them in the most obscure corners, nooks, and crannies of the establishment. As people cleaned equipment and other areas of the restaurant, they collected the dots and redeemed them with the manager for some sort of prize or recognition. The more they collected, the better the reward. (Also see "Get the Point(s).")

The idea behind this was to start getting people to look in places they would normally pass over or ignore and to use positive reinforcement of proper behavior, rather than just punishing the absence of proper behavior. The employees never knew when these dots might appear. However, it didn't take them too long to notice that they tended to appear right before a health department inspector showed up. Finally, if any dots were overlooked, this created an excellent opportunity for feedback and training for improvement.

## #79 Mystery Mess

This is a variation on "Collect the Dots." "Mystery Mess" is done by either creating clutter or marking existing clutter with a prize sticker. Now, you're probably thinking, why in the world would you want to create more mess than already exists, or, even better, why not just pick up the existing clutter yourself instead of marking it and leaving it? Because the objective is not just to clean up the mess. It is to get others (besides the boss) into the habit of looking for and cleaning up messes.

If people never know whether there might be a prize underneath a mess, they're more likely to pick up messes that they might otherwise have ignored or walked around. Again, this is merely another fun and positive way to keep people thinking and acting on your behalf because they want to, not just because they have to.

## #80 Whaddaya Know?

Like it or not, know it or not, your employees are playing games at work. Whether it's a game of computer solitaire or some other diversion, you might as well just acknowledge it and capitalize upon it. As a footnote, it has been proven that periodic downtime is both therapeutic and necessary, particularly for people in mentally demanding and stressful occupations. For many, the Internet has replaced the traditional water cooler.

One way to capitalize on this new gaming mentality is to create your own internal, customized crossword puzzles, anagrams, and other word games that are both challenging and educational. You can incorporate product information, little-known facts about the company, or any other content that both entertains and educates. Like other ideas, this one also dovetails well with a contest for prizes or other recognition.

If you have the capability and budget, you might even want to create your own computer games and other diversionary activities for people to use instead of the ones that come prebundled or off the Internet. If they're going to play, make it pay.

You may have policies regarding the use of company computers for games and recreation, but I hate to break the news to you, they are usually futile and tend to have a more negative impact on morale than just measuring for results and trusting people to do what's right. No matter how tightly a company tries to regulate and police behavior, there is always going to be a certain amount of "system slop" that people will find and use. In fact, the tighter it gets, the greater the need! Whether it's trashcan basketball or just doodling, there are workplace games that people must play to stay sane and to feel some modicum of freedom. The bottom line is: Are your employees doing the job? If they are, get over it!

Along the same lines as the crossword puzzle, another idea involves training in product or service knowledge, but not just as a game. Rather, the purpose is to teach product, service, or other company or competitor knowledge using the touch-tones on the telephone, or via the computer.

Typically, this concept has been used most often for salespeople, who are expected to know the latest information about what they are selling and how it compares to the competition. At the end of each quiz, the employees should be able to get their scores immediately, and they should also be able to take a retest until they reach a satis-factory score. The advantage of doing this via telephone or computer is that people who are on the road can take their quizzes anytime, anyplace, and in complete privacy. This is also known as programmed learning or instruction.

"Whaddaya Know?" can be both fun and educational. Not only is it important for people to know the company's products and ser-vices, but most strong cultures also rely on stories, history, symbols, and even fables. Although these may be covered in new employee ori-entation programs, retention is minimal, and the mechanism for imparting this information is usually ineffective. Plus, everyone can use a refresher course every once in a while.

Although the most common subject matter is current product and service information, this procedure could be adapted to many of the other ideas in this book, including such things as trivia contests. The telephone/computer response option makes the procedure easy, immediate, and inexpensive. Some companies do this on an ongoing basis, allowing people to accumulate points over time for various lev-els of recognition and reward, which encourages continued partici-pation and learning (see "Get the Point[s]").

You can change the theme of each contest to cover a different subject, from the founding history of the company, to little-known facts, to customer knowledge, to new product/service launches, to funny facts about individuals and their hobbies, past lives, and other ways to get to know them beyond their job title (also see "Getting to Know You"). People remember more when they learn through voluntary, fun, and positive ways, and trivia contests can provide a vehicle to make it happen.

# #81 Reverse Mentoring

We are in an era in which our children know more than we do about *some* things. One of those is technology. Another is the ability to adapt to change. Can you think of any oth-ers? The same is true for new employees versus "old" ones.

Without going into a dissertation on generational and demographic influences and differences, if you translate this to the workplace, would it not make sense to capitalize on the fresh, current knowledge and skills of your entry-level new hires? That's what reverse mentoring is.

Let's face it, in today's world, it doesn't take very long for someone to become personally obsolete. So, as you bring "new" people into your organization, look at the skill sets and attitudes that they are bringing with them, and create ways to "teach the elders" what these skills and attitudes are and why they are valuable. This is no different from any other mentoring process; it's just upside down.

And if your "senior citizens" are resistant to this concept or if their egos are too fragile to acknowledge the value of youth, you and they have a bigger problem that needs to be addressed. Neither they nor the organization can afford the luxury of stagnation.

I just bristle whenever I hear a resistor say something like "I'm just not good with computers." That's just an easy way for them to cop out of their responsibility to adapt to the times. Did they say, "I'm not good with televisions," when they were introduced? Did they say, "I'm not good with microwave ovens?" Of course not! Because they saw the personal benefits as well as the personal downside of resisting these new technologies. In "Reverse Mentoring," you will find out very quickly which employees are compatible with a learning organization philosophy. It also communicates to your newest recruits that you value them too.

This doesn't have to be insulting or demeaning to your seniors. It could be done in a workshop or group setting, if that is more palatable. New employees could teach a class on the latest technology or software application. Or, you could even have a roundtable discussion on differences in perception or other attitudinal topics (generational, philosophical, etc.). At the very least, you could *ask the elders* what they would like to learn or know from the newest crop of talent. Not to do this is to waste a valuable resource that you are paying for anyway. Make it a win-win proposition!

# #82 Training Theater

Although most people have been exposed to skits and role-plays of one kind or another, this idea is a skit with a learning point for the audience. Rather than just telling people what to do or how to do it, "Training Theater" really drives it home.

It's easier just to give you an example. That same friend I referred to in "Collect the Dots" who owned several upscale fast-food restaurants (which means that they were located in nice malls and food courts and were overpriced) had monthly staff meetings. But he didn't call them staff meetings. He called them cast parties, following the Disney philosophy of language.

Most members of his workforce were immature, inexperienced, and in some cases troubled teens. He also encouraged the employees to interact with the customers while prepping, cooking, and presenting the food order, to involve the customer in the process and thus reduce the perceived waiting time and turn it into more of an entertainment experience.

It came to my friend's attention that some of the male employees were going a little beyond being friendly and actually crossing into inappropriate sexual innuendoes. His first reaction may have been to read them the riot act, but instead he taught them a lesson through "Training Theater."

At the next cast party, he and a couple of store managers got together ahead of time and dressed in full drag as women—the heels, the hose, the lipstick, the works! A couple of other people played the part of the male employees. They then proceeded to act out "how not to treat women" at his restaurants, with the actors making all kinds of similarly inappropriate remarks to each other, "hey babying it up" and generally making fools of themselves.

After the laughter had died down and the boss got out of drag, they discussed what they had just witnessed. Without pointing fingers at anyone individually, the message was powerfully conveyed and respectfully received because of the way in which it was communicated. In this case, the boss was even willing to demean himself to send an important message. Ironically, he was actually respected even more for addressing the issue in this way. No one was publicly lynched, the boss was willing to let down his guard, and the message was heard (seen) loudly and clearly.

If acting isn't for you, consider hiring a local improvisational theater group to do it for you. Just about every community has a theater group or acting students who can take your concept and run with it. If all else fails, go to a local entertainment or talent agency and tell them what you are trying to accomplish. This may cost a little more, but it does work. Role-playing has been used for years, but "Training Theater" takes it one step further, particularly if the boss can make a fool of himself or herself in the process. Even serious learning can be fun.

# #83 Road Trip

This idea can have many variations, but the essence of it is to get people out of their physical boxes to see another world. You might visit a competitor's store to see how that competitor does what you do. You might visit an unrelated business that is known for exemplary service to see what might be transferable to yours. You might take technical people to see how your end product is sold or used. You might take manufacturing people to see the raw materials suppliers.

I first tried this with a luxury auto dealer. Recognizing that this was as much a retail environment as a hotel, department store, etc., we identified the key attributes of any retail shopping experience. These were things like personal interaction, store philosophy, ambiance, merchandise display, and customer service. We then surveyed people with the demographics of those who buy luxury cars to determine what other retailers they held in high regard, and two that came up repeatedly were Nordstrom and the Ritz-Carlton Hotel. Unfortunately, neither of these retailers was in the dealer's market area. So, we took a field trip.

We put together a cross section of employees, jumped in a van, drove across state lines, and experienced these retailers ourselves. Without belaboring the issue, these employees returned with a new attitude about service and what was possible. They transferred their learning from a different retail environment to theirs. Things like the Ritz-Carlton Credo (guiding principles), the ten-foot rule (acknowledging any customer within ten feet of you), and the morning line-up (quickie daily meetings) could raise the bar so that they could provide even better customer service.

As you can see, the options are endless. Sometimes just getting a fresh perspective alone is invaluable. Make the trip fun. Rent a bus, have snacks and beverages, and cap it off with a gathering to discuss their experiences and findings and how they can use this information to be more effective or successful. Then have these employees share their discoveries with others, perhaps in an all-employee meeting. Don't lose the learning.

## #84 Silo Destruction

As organizations grow, new departments spring up and old ones expand. More and more walls go up, both physically and mentally. Before you know it, it's as if people were working in silos. Just envision a whole bunch of tall, narrow buildings (departments), each of which is shut off from the ones next to it. Eventually, no one knows much about what goes on outside their own walls, nor do people appreciate how what they do affects others, nor do they care, and vice versa. Isolation and insulation are the final refuges of bureaucracy.

Once every month or so, have a different department host an open house for everyone else in the organization. This should include a narrated guided tour of the department, along with handouts, rosters of names and jobs (also see "Public Resumes"), and anything else that will help educate people on what the department does, how it affects others, what the department needs from others in order to do a better job, and the added value. A department could even ask its internal customers how it could serve them better. (Also see "Corporation Compensation.")

If you don't want to tie up a lot of people giving tours, do what many museums do and make the tour self-guided, with either a taped narration or placards describing what goes on as people walk through. Obviously, the personal touch is better, though.

Food and beverage is always a plus. Give out small gifts, like a mouse pad or a coffee mug or something, to encourage attendance and participation. At one company, we rented a cotton candy machine. It didn't take long for people to notice the smell and then see others walking the halls with sticky faces and fingers. No one likes to see someone else getting something for free that he or she didn't. Make it something that the grapevine will pick up and support. People are cheap and so are these ideas. (See "Sales Tagalongs" and "Do Your Workwork!" for other ways of breaking down barriers.)

Since an ounce of prevention is worth a pound of cure, let's talk about a way to keep silos from forming in the first place. One is to redesign your work spaces so that departments are not segregated to begin with. Small companies don't usually have this problem because initially everyone is working pretty much side by side. But then expansion sets in, walls go up, new floors are added, departments are created, and turf lines form.

Follow the lead of Bolt, Inc., a New York–based teen-communication platform. They went from fifteen people working out of a small office, with everyone sitting together, to hundreds of people occupying space on several floors. They started to lose their sense of oneness. Their goal was to revive the small company, all-together feeling, so they developed what they call the "hive-mind" seating system. In this scenario, a sales rep might be sitting next to an accountant who might be sitting next to a programmer, and the ankle bone's connected to the shin bone, and the….

If you decide to try this work arrangement, do not exclude anyone. At Bolt, executives are sitting next to everyone else. But what about privacy, you may ask. Ever hear of a conference room?

This approach resulted in people knowing one another on a first-name basis, everyone understanding what everyone else does and how it fits in, no us versus them mentalities, and better brainstorming activity.

If you don't have silos yet, try to prevent building them. And, if silos have already reared their ugly walls, destroy them now!

# #85 Sales Tagalongs

Related to the "Ambassadors, Advocates, and Apostles" (AAA) idea is the concept of taking nonsalespeople on sales calls. Although AAA is intended to encourage everyone to be a salesperson for the company, "Sales Tagalongs" also exposes people to the process with an experienced sales professional.

However, the payoff for "Sales Tagalongs" goes beyond just additional sales and sales training. If you include technical people, development people, administrative people, and really just about any other nonsales employees, they will also develop a more intimate appreciation for the people they are ultimately serving, regardless of their jobs. And, as a side benefit, they may also come to realize that your sales force doesn't have such a cushy job after all.

An extension of this idea is to take employees to visit *end users* of your products or services as well. If your customer is not the end user, the "End-User Tagalong" will show employees how the customer is affected by your product or service and put a real-life face on the impersonal database. It may also spark new ideas for additional product and service improvements and enhancements, particularly after seeing firsthand how the customer uses (or doesn't use) them. In fact, the tagalong idea in general could be applied to any department, function, or person. If exposing employees to a process would be beneficial, just do it. It might be particularly valuable for an intern experience (see "Monica"). See "Silo Destruction" and "Cooperation Compensation" for additional ways to break down interdepartmental barriers.

# #86 Practice Makes Perfect

One of my most valuable and interesting client experiences was to sit in a cubicle beside a customer service representative, wearing a telephone headset, and listening in on just one day's worth of customer complaints and problems and hear how they were handled (or not).

Taking this a step further, one client started tape recording customer complaint calls. Before returning the call, this client sat down with a group of trainees, who listened to each call and then discussed and practiced how they would handle each particular situation. Then, someone would actually handle the call and they would all debrief it. Real life, real time, real experience. There is no better training.

# #87 KISS

Some of the most powerful messages are the simplest ones. Have you ever read the fine print in some of the contests and campaigns that companies sponsor? It makes your head swim and detracts from the intended fun. If the contest is just more work, people won't want to bother with it. Also, the more difficult it is to understand the *rules* (what a great choice of words for something that is intended to be fun), the less belief there will be that the goal is attainable. Keep it simple, stupid (KISS)!

Pick a theme, then create a very simple but memorable logo or slogan and put it on a button, on coffee mugs, on pens, on mouse pads, or even on yourself in the form of a temporary tattoo. It doesn't need to be understandable at first glance. In fact, it may even be better if people have to ask what it means.

For example, Bertholon-Rowland (a Pittsburgh, Pennsylvania, benefits consulting firm) has as its company motto "It's My Job!"

**Figure 6-1**

New hires are given a button to wear that says exactly that above the company logo (Figure 6-1). During orientation, it is made clear that one of the company's driving values is to do whatever it takes to satisfy the customer. Have you ever gone to a store and searched out a clerk to ask a question, only to be told, "That's not my department"? Or, have you ever had a complaint or problem and been told that you will have to come back later to talk to a manager? Doesn't that make you feel a lot better?

Along those same lines, Bertholon-Rowland does not want to hear anyone muttering the words "That's not my job." Not only does the button drive the message home to the new hire, but more senior employees see the new people wearing these buttons and are continually reminded of this guiding principle as well. It also lets more senior employees know that these are new employees and that they should welcome them, show them around, and make them feel comfortable.

**Figure 6-2**

Another example of a theme that begged the question "What does that mean?" comes from a company that encouraged risk taking and trying new things.

The company's theme button was the picture in Figure 6-2.

Obviously, people would ask what it meant. The company's answer was that it was symbolic for "put your butt on the line!" This was a simple, fun, and somewhat irreverent way to remind people of what was important. Unfortunately, another company with quite a different culture took the idea and turned it upside down (see Figure 6-3). This came to mean, "Cover your _ _ _!"

**Figure 6-3**

Figures 6-4 through 6-6 show a few more "KISS" button themes. See if you can figure out the larger objective of the companies that used them.*

Get the idea? Whatever you come up with, make sure it is consistent with the culture or change objective you are trying to cultivate. If it isn't believable, the purpose will have been defeated because people will make a mockery of it. Also, when using an acronym like BMG, be sure that there isn't a real obvious alternative that may be obscene, contradictory, or counterproductive to your intended purpose. It's not a big deal, but if you thought of it right away, someone else will too.

Figure 6-4            Figure 6-5

Figure 6-6

# #88 Share the Wealth of Knowledge

I started this idea when I founded the Pennsylvania Speakers Association, a chapter of the National Speakers Association, but it is easily adaptable to any group. Since most people join professional associations to further their knowledge and careers, they also tend to purchase self-improvement tapes, books, and other resources to keep current and promote their self-development.

However, few people listen to, read, or otherwise use these resources more than once or twice before they start to gather dust

---

* Figure 6-4: No bitchin', moanin', or groanin'! Figure 6-5: Not what you want to hear during a major change effort. Figure 6-6: I think you can figure this one out on your own!

or are relegated to their personal archives, i.e., a box in the attic, basement, or garage.

Why not ask people in your organization to loan or donate their tapes, books, and other resources to a common library for use by others? You will be absolutely amazed at how quickly your library comes to be overflowing with really great stuff. Then designate someone to compile a menu of what's available and send it to everyone. But allow only those people who have donated something to borrow something. The price of a library card is at least one donation to the library.

On a related but somewhat different note, have you ever gotten really sick of seeing the same old magazines at your doctor's or dentist's office, or one of the many other "waiting" rooms you are forced to frequent? Why not survey your people to see what magazines they subscribe to and whether they would be willing to bring them in when they are done with them. Most people throw away the previous issues of the most popular magazines every month, or just pile them in a heap somewhere to collect dust until the next paper drive comes along.

Not only could your lobby be a gold mine of great reading materials, but you could also put magazine racks in your lunchroom or other common areas where employees and customers could enjoy them. This is yet another free but valuable way to recycle the diversity of resources that are right at your fingertips.

## #89 Irreverence and Irrelevance

One of the key ways to keep good people is to provide them with constant learning and growth opportunities. Traditionally this has meant training and development, which also meant that it covered purely job skills. In the spirit of "Food for Thought," this idea extends more to the individual's interests and needs for mental diversion. Even though it may be fun and beneficial (and inexpensive) to teach everyone the latest dance craze at lunch, remember that you have hired a vast collection of diverse people, not a homogenous mass of clones. Diverse people have diverse needs.

Consider providing some *individualized* learning and growth opportunities. Whether this is done only as a perk for special performance or as a standard benefit for everyone, you will reap major rewards in employee morale, enthusiasm, and loyalty if people's life interests beyond the job are supported.

Everyone talks about the benefits of living a balanced life, but employers fail to recognize that the job is only one of the weights on the scale, and the more one-sided our emphasis on purely job-related learning, the more tilted the scale. Employees at American Century of Kansas City, Missouri, have life-cycle accounts that cover wellness, fitness, and "personal" development—like guitar lessons!

If someone is interested in learning a job skill beyond the ones he or she is using now, why not support it? It may keep that person in your company. If you don't, the person might have to leave to fulfill it. Some companies support learning a foreign language in exchange for letting the company use it when needed, e.g., foreign visitors, correspondence, etc. (Also see "Brainpower Inventory.")

Employees' interests may have nothing to do with a job skill at all. They may want to learn to fly (not literally, I hope), or to kayak, or to ski. Why not allocate a certain percentage of your training and development budget to support non-job-related, but healthful learning?

You don't have to devote your entire training and development budget to fun stuff, but you can use some of it for personal well-being. Weigh that cost against the cost of unbalanced, unproductive, and ultimately unemployed people and you will quickly see that it is an investment, not a cost.

## #90 Read between the Lines

Have you ever given someone a book or an article to read? Whether you did this merely as a thoughtful gesture or as an assignment, do you ever wonder if that person actually read it? Here is a kind way to find out.

The next time you give someone something to read, find an obscure place toward the end of the publication where you can write in the inner margin or some other inconspicuous place. Then, write a personal message in the margin, such as, "I hope you are enjoying this book. Now that you have made it this far, give me a call and I'll take you to lunch to discuss it."

Try to use a positive comment and an incentive so that it doesn't come across as a test. If the person never calls, you know she or he never read it. The downside of this idea is that you can do it only once per person. After the first time, if it is successful, the person will start to look for the message, which defeats the purpose.

If it truly is a test and the publication is mandatory reading, you shouldn't need to do this. Just have a meeting to discuss it. But if it was a gift or just a kind thought, this is a nice way to share the knowledge with a little perk along the way.

# #91 Getting to Know You

Whether you are planning a party and want people to really get to know one another, just wanting to generate interesting conversation with a friend, conducting an interview, or trying to build a team at work, there are several techniques that can be both fun and insightful.

The first one is called The Four E's. I have used it very successfully as an initial get-acquainted exercise for people at work. It is truly amazing how people can work together for years and know relatively little about one another (also see "Public Resumes"). As I used it in my counseling practice and in training people to interview better, the Four E's was merely a mental structure for people to follow in responding to the age-old inquiry "Tell me about yourself." The format is shown in Figure 6-7.

This may look like an awfully long structure for the answer to a simple question ("Tell me about yourself"), but depending on the context and the purpose (i.e., whether it is merely an icebreaker or is to truly get to know people in some depth), you can set a time limit for responses. In counseling, our goal was to get it down to two minutes or less.

## Getting to Know You!
### (The 4 E's)

**1 Early Life**

- Where from?
- Unique characteristic(s)
- Significant accomplishment
- Defining moment/event
- Growing pains/lessons

**2 Education**

- Where?
- What?
- Why?
- Significant accomplishment
- Defining moment/event

**3 Experience(s)**

- Work
- Nonwork
- Transitions
- Significant accomplishment
- Defining moment/event

**4 Expectations**

- Plans for future
- Three fun things I would like to do before I die are...
- Hopes/dreams/goals
- Anything at all

**Figure 6-7**

In fact, the best way to set the tone and the pace is for you to go first. Teach by doing. Once you show that it is both painless and interesting, the doors open for others to share their stories; and they will.

Also, do not make it a requirement that every item be covered. The items listed under each E are merely thought starters and mental prompts. Do, however, ask that everyone say something about each of the periods represented by the E's (Early life, Education, Experience and Expectations, i.e., the future), and do them in order. This creates a chronology of thought that pulls from the past, leads to the present, and projects to the future. I have never done this exercise without being positively surprised at how people open up. And someone will invariably say, "Wow, I didn't know that about you!"

A great example of this took place at PeopleSoft when the company decided to put its own people in some of its recruitment ads. The intention was to show the company's employees as Renaissance types and to demonstrate their diversity of talent and experience. In the process PeopleSoft found not only that it had an employee who had won a gold medal for synchronized swimming in the Olympics, but that there were actually several other Olympians among the employees.

Another "Getting to Know You" exercise is to ask people to finish various sentences, such as:

"People would be surprised to know that I. . ."

"An accomplishment I am most proud of is. . ."

"My first job was. . ."

"One of my secret vices is. . ."

"Three words that would best describe me are. . ."

"My idea of a dream vacation would be. . ."

"One thing I would like to do before I die is. . ."

"One thing I could really do without is. . ."

"If I could have dinner with anyone in the world, it would be. . ."

"If I could go back in time, I would go to (where and when?)."

"A movie that I would watch any time is. . ."

"If they made a movie about my life, I would like the actor who plays me to be. . ."

"If I had a personal theme song, it would be. . ."

"Three things that you would always find in my refrigerator are..."

"One of my biggest pet peeves is..."

You can make up any questions you wish, but ideally the questions should reveal something about the person that most people would not have known. You can also go around the room as many times as you want until you run out of surprising revelations, or until someone screams or hits you. In fact, the questions don't even have to be deep or contemplative. I have seen the following "What is?" format spark a very lively and fun interchange. What is:

"Your nickname?"

"Your favorite TV show?" (Why?)

"On your mousepad?"

"Your favorite smell?"

"Your worst feeling?"

"Your best feeling?"

"The first thing you think of when you wake in the morning?"

"Your favorite Web site?"

"Your vice?"

"Your scariest moment?"

"Your most embarrassing moment?"

"Your pet's(s') name(s)?" (Why?)

A variation on "Finish the sentence" is called "Two truths and a lie." In this case, each person says three things about himself or herself that most people wouldn't know—but one of them is a lie. The participants must guess which statement is the lie. The outcome is similar to that of "Finish the sentence" but this technique allows people to have some fun with their fantasies and to trick one another in the process.

Again, these techniques can be used either in a social setting or as part of a workplace exercise. The reason they are particularly powerful at work is that when people start to get to know one another beyond the job, they also start to realize that they are all human and that they have other interests, backgrounds, experiences, and challenges (past and present) that transcend the day-to-day. This builds camaraderie, empathy, and trust. Just try it!

# #92 Put Your Money Where Your Mouth Is!

This idea might also be called, *there ain't no such thing as free speech*. Choice of language, terminology, and other lingo can have a significant effect on behavior, particularly in the workplace. "Put Your Money Where Your Mouth Is!" is a way to reinforce language by making people pay when they mess up.

As a consultant and professional speaker, I have had to become hypersensitive to language and learn my clients' terminology quickly if I was to connect and succeed with them. Until you learn the language, you are an outsider.

One long-term client of mine insisted that the culture change effort we were working on be called a process and not a program. What this client was trying to emphasize was that programs have a beginning and an end, but a process is ongoing. Programs also tend to get a bad rap because most people have been programmed to death, with no real apparent benefit. So, whenever anyone called the culture change effort a program, he or she had to put a buck in a jar. When the amount of money in the jar got to a certain level, the money was used for something that was fun for everyone, like a pizza party. Another organization did the same thing, but donated the money to a children's charity. Where the money goes is less important than why it is collected in the first place.

Language affects behavior. Choice of words is connected to thought, which is connected to behavior. Most people have heard about the Disney culture and how Disney has successfully maintained it over the years. What they may not know is that Disney is adamant about using the proper language and terminology. They aren't rides; they're attractions. They aren't customers; they're guests. They aren't on duty; they're on stage. They aren't uniforms; they're costumes. They aren't employees; they are cast members. You don't go to Personnel; you go to Central Casting, and so on.

Think about how your perspective changes when you realize you are "on stage." Suddenly you are a performer, not just a worker. Wouldn't it be great if all your employees "performed"? This idea can be used for any initiative in which you are trying to encourage or discourage certain words.

On the "discourage" side, I have seen this idea used to get people to clean up their language, i.e., to not swear. Whatever your objective, "Put Your Money Where Your Mouth Is!" is a positive way to influence language and behavior in the workplace.

# #93 Wanted: Dead or Achieved!

There's something to be said for public notices and motivation. If you commit to doing something in front of others, you are more likely to follow through and do it. Call it peer pressure, call it embarrassment, or call it pride, it just works. That's why I recommend ending each meeting with a written commitment statement or list of things that people said they would do, who committed to do each of them, and by what date. Then, distribute the list and copy the boss. But take this idea even further.

Make it a standard procedure for everyone in your organization or department to *post* her or his most important "to-do" on the office or cubicle wall or even on a central bulletin board once a month. Not the whole "to-do" list, because no one ever gets everything done and no one really cares that Joe plans to reorganize his files, or that Mary wants to go shopping for a new plant. Just the important stuff.

If the "to-do" is too big to get done in a month, this is a great way to teach people how to break big projects into incremental chunks, and to actually get them done. This procedure is not intended to lead to a public lynching or to be a mutual embarrassment contest. Each person picks his or her own "to-do." Fair enough?

The interesting phenomenon is that most people will aim rather high, because they do not want to look like lightweights or they want others to see what important stuff they have to do. Just be sure that everyone checks his or her item off at the end of the month and puts up a new one for the next month (or puts the same one back up, but in a different color to designate that it is being recycled).

To-do's posted for the first time could be in green, for "Go." Carryovers could be in yellow, for "Caution" or "Coward." And if the to-do still isn't done by the third month, it turns red for "Stop!" This technique not only creates a bias for action, but also educates everyone about what others are doing (or *not* doing). It may even cause some to pitch in and help, if it is something in which they are interested, from which they might benefit, or something they may already be working on too. (Also see "Wish List.")

**ASSIGNMENT:** Now get out your own "to-do" list (or make a special "weird ideas list") and start identifying which ideas from this book you are going to implement. Commit to at least one per month, and post it in your office. If anyone else in your company or department is reading this book, make this a requirement. Make it a contest. Use the ideas in this book to make the ideas happen. Circulate the lists among the other readers. Put together a peer pressure team for weird ideas. Are you getting the idea?

# WeIRD IDeAS FOR ENHANCING YOUR CoMPANY IMAGE

## aka SALES, SERVICE, PUBLIC RELATIONS, & PERSONAL SATISFACTION

*This category of ideas is the shortest in length but the broadest in scope. You will find ideas ranging from mystery shopping to customer relations to personal fulfillment to feeding the hungry. Bottom line: these are ideas that defied prior categorization but deserved inclusion. I hope you find them useful and valuable.*

# #94 Gorilla Shopping

This is a particularly effective technique for improving awareness of your brand in the minds of the salespeople at the retailer or reseller store level. It is similar to mystery shopping, but in this case, you are mystery shopping your own products where they are supposed to be displayed and sold.

I first saw this done at the former MECC (Minnesota Educational Computing Corporation), an educational software company which was trying to compete for valuable retail shelf space and name recognition in a quagmire of products. The company called it "Gorilla Shopping" (as opposed to "Guerrilla Shopping") because one of the main characters in one of its most popular programs was, in fact, a gorilla, and one of the side prizes was a giant stuffed gorilla.

They created a contest within the company in which everyone was encouraged to participate. Employees would pick up a "Gorilla Visit" slip to complete each time they conducted a campaign. The campaign could be carried out either by telephone or in person. The slips would then be entered into a sweepstakes for a periodic drawing for a prize. The more you did, the better your odds of winning. Again, this is pay for performance with purposeful fun (also see "Get the Point[s]").

Because the marketing department did not expect everyone to be adept at mystery shopping, it created a campaign briefing sheet, with sample scripts and everything else needed to complete the task successfully. Here is a sample of a telephone campaign sheet for one of the company's math educational software programs:

**YOUR MISSION**

Pretend you are shopping for (product name)

**YOUR OBJECTIVE**

1. Get a store salesperson to spend some time with the product.

2. Get them to read you things off the box over the phone.

3. Use this time to "sell" (product name).

### WHY?

**1.** (product name) needs a little help. As a new product, it is getting "lost" in the onslaught of other programs on the market.

**2.** We need to gain "mind-share" (a fancy marketing term that simply means "attention") of the retail salespeople.

**3.** A phone call should only take a few minutes of your time.

**4.** This is a way of taking "Gorilla Marketing" outside of the local market. You'll be calling stores all over the country.

**5.** It's sneaky, underhanded, and of questionable ethics...which is why the Marketing Department wholly endorses it. *[This was said in jest, as a dig at Marketing.]*

### METHODS

**Step 1:** Pick up a form listing 4 retail stores that should carry (product name) Forms can be found at the front desk, near the big, stuffed, banana-eating mammal (i.e., Gorilla marketing).

**Step 2:** Call them at your leisure during the day. Our advice is to make the call at times when you think they are not very busy, i.e., during the week, from 10:00 A.M. to 12:00 P.M., and 2:00 P.M. to 4:00 P.M. (their time).

**Step 3:** Be yourself, but act like you're looking specifically for (product name).

**Step 4:** Follow suggested script, but adapt to your own peculiar and lovable style. See attached script.

**Step 5:** After you make 4 phone calls, hand in the form and you'll be entered into the Gorilla contest.

**Step 6:** Pick up another form with 4 new stores. Go to it again, and get another chance at the big prize.

### POSSIBLE SCRIPTS

**VOLUNTEER:** Hi, I just read a great review of a new program in *Family PC* magazine, and it sounds perfect for my child. It's called *(product name)*. Does your store carry it?

*or,*

Hi, my kid just came back from school and all he can talk about is this new program they're using at the school called *(product name)*. Does your store carry it?

*or,*

Hi, I recently received a demo disk for a program called *(product name)*. My kids absolutely love it, and I want to buy the full program. Does your store carry it?

*or,*

My kid plays this software game called *(product name)* at a friend's house. It's all he talks about, so I think I want to get it for him for Christmas. Does your store carry it?

**SALESPERSON:** I think we do.

**VOLUNTEER:** Can you get it off the shelf and read to me what it says on the box?

**SALESPERSON:** Yeah, hold on one minute…here we go…(and the clerk proceeds to read the story line)

**VOLUNTEER:** That sounds fun. What kind of math does it cover?

**SALESPERSON:** It says "Addition, subtraction, multiplication and division. Whole numbers, fractions, decimals and percentages. There are story problems and something about 60 levels of difficulty."

**VOLUNTEER:** That sounds fun, and great for my ten-year old. Who makes it?

**SALESPERSON:** I don't know. It says something like "_____."

**VOLUNTEER:** Oh, _____. They're the people who make _____ and _____. My kids love their software. *(product name)* sounds great. What's the price?

**SALESPERSON:** $XX.XX

**VOLUNTEER:** That's a good deal. What time are you open 'til tonight?

**SALESPERSON:** Until 9 p.m.. Do you want me to put it aside for you?

**VOLUNTEER:** No, that's okay. I'm going to check a couple more places first. Thanks for your help. Bye!

There were also instructions for conducting personal store visits, including asking for a demo disk, asking for prices if they aren't posted on the shelf, asking about the company's products that the store doesn't carry, asking about whether the store has "demo days," etc.

The Gorilla Shoppers were also instructed to report back to marketing about competitors' promotions, to grab samples, and to ask about any missing company products (i.e., empty spaces where products should be).

Whatever twist you want to put on this concept, it is a fun and very effective way to turn everyone into a marketer and ambassador for your products, and it saves money on third-party mystery shopping services.

# #95 Customer Appreciation Days

This is somewhat related to "Break the Mold," but it is focused exclusively on appreciating the customer and attracting attention while doing it. Find a way to make a splash, and, even better, find a way to get some free media attention out of it. Here's an example:

One convenience store/gas station decided that they would hold a customer appreciation day. They rented tuxedos for all the attendants, and to draw a crowd, the promotion offered everyone full-service gas at the self-service price for the entire day. There were free popcorn, token gifts, and a lot of hoopla. The store also advertised this promotion in advance, and, as you might expect, it was particularly packed during the morning and evening commuter drive times.

Now, here's the added punch. Because of the drive-time crunch, the morning and evening radio and TV traffic helicopters reported the logjam. They also investigated the "problem" and proceeded to tell the entire listening/viewing audience that it was due to a customer appreciation event at _____ and that the attendants were dressed in top hats and tails and that full-serve gas was being sold at self-serve prices. Thank you very much! You can't buy that kind of advertising.

Think about how you can generate free press for doing something good while also generating customer loyalty in the process. Don't do the same old trite things, like dressing up as a giant chicken and waving to passersby. Or renting a giant balloon. Who cares? And what does that do for the customer? For its hundredth anniversary, J. M. Smucker, the jam and jelly maker, invited everybody in Orrville, Ohio (the company's headquarters), for a pancake breakfast. More than 20,000 people were served.

I have also seen upscale and luxury car dealers throw a top-shelf buffet or catered event in the showroom, complete with strolling violins or some other entertainment throughout the day or evening. The dealers obviously invite current customers, but they also allow each customer to bring a guest (i.e., a prospective customer) and his or her family, to pig out for free—of course, in the showroom alongside all the latest new models. An important detail: Be sure to use posh, classy invitations, similar to the ones you would see for a fancy wedding, with linen paper stock, RSVP card, etc.

If an event like this is announced and scheduled properly, many busy people who don't want to cook for themselves, do dishes, etc., will come for a purely self-serving reason—a free meal! What do you care, as long as you are increasing customer loyalty, getting good press, and being introduced to new prospects? It's good for employees, too.

Also, if you can get (or even pay) a celebrity guest to attend, your chances of getting some free press increases even more. Maybe you can get a local sports hero (past or present), a media personality, or an actor or musician or artist. Whatever type of celebrity you decide on, be sure to issue a news release far enough in advance of the event to make it easy for the media to be there. Whatever you do, make a scene and get noticed.

## #96 Customer Clinics

Whether you sell software or automobiles, you can find ways to make your product or service more valuable to your customers and increase loyalty and sales at the same time. How? By educating your customers on how to use what you sell.

Software companies sponsor user conferences where techies and other customers and users can commiserate about their experiences, network, and socialize while finding out how to use the product more effectively and efficiently. They can also ask questions and offer suggestions, which in turn may help the developers make improvements that will ultimately allow the company to sell even more. Attendees may even have the opportunity to earn a certification, which has added value to their organization when they return. Certification in the use of a particular brand of product increases the probability that the person will continue to use it. It's also an ego booster.

Some automobile dealerships have new car customer clinics to introduce customers to the dealership, its personnel, its procedures, and its departments, and to review both routine and other types of maintenance and repair requirements. They may also show customers how to do simple maintenance items themselves, like checking the oil, tire pressures, and safety items.

Guests can also bring friends and family, who wander around the showroom, drooling over the newest models and thinking how nice this dealership is to offer such free services. There is usually food and beverages, and perhaps a token gift, preferably one that will bring people back to the dealership again, like a free lube and oil and filter change or a discount on some other needed service or product.

Software companies may extend the free upgrade period for user-conference attendees or give them a demo disk of an upcoming program. Or, they may ask customers to beta-test a yet-to-be-released product in exchange for a discount on the product when it is released. The customers are getting a scoop on something new, and the company is getting customer input, feedback, and loyalty, which will help it to sell even more. The rewards for loyalty can breed even more loyalty.

The more a customer knows about how to use your product or service, the more likely that customer is to remain loyal to it, and to you. Just about any type of product or service will lend itself to a clinic or conference. The point is to educate your customers about the features and benefits of doing business with you, rather than with someone else, and to help them use what you sell. Wrap it around an upbeat event, with food and beverage and maybe even some entertainment or takeaways (i.e., freebies), and it's added value to them and increased customer loyalty and goodwill for you.

"Customer Clinics" are also an opportunity for you to let your customers know what's coming in the way of improvements, specials, or any other hooks to keep them coming back for more. But please be subtle about making any kind of sales pitch during one of these clinics or conferences. This is to be positioned as a free benefit or a value-added activity, not a captive marketing ploy. The best marketing and public relations is that which happens without people knowing it. Once you have built a loyal customer base, they will want to know these things. You won't have to shove it down their throats.

## #97 Greeters and Minglers

Have you ever gone to visit someone in the hospital? Although this idea has relevance in all kinds of environments, when I think about the most confusing places to visit, it's the hospital that comes to mind first. You usually have to follow a bunch of colored lines or dots on the floor, go to other floors and wings, and maybe take more than one elevator—not to mention the fear of walking into a trauma unit or into the wrong room. And you're just not in the mood for learning your way through a maze.

Rather than just handing someone a card or a map and pointing the way, why not have a greeter/mingler take people who need help where they want to go? Hospitals, especially, use more volunteers than just about any type of organization, so there's no reason why they couldn't use some students or seniors or other charitable group to welcome visitors and escort them to their destinations while talking to them on the way. The escorts would offer peace of mind and literal hand-holding to distressed or confused visitors. The hospital could also make major points in public relations, not to mention preventing a bunch of strangers from groping down the wrong halls.

This same principle could be used, perhaps to a lesser extent, in other organizations. The mingler part of the concept is intended to shorten the perceived waiting time by having someone to occupy the time and attention of the customer or visitor. I have seen this technique used very successfully in doctors', dentists', and other medical providers' offices, where the greeters also helped seniors and language/literacy-challenged people to complete their forms and helped to get everything in order so that the office visit would run more smoothly. After all, who are the forms really for? They aren't for the patient. They're for you. So, why make the first part of the experience both negative and threatening for your customer?

On a more mundane level, the greeter/mingler idea has been used by organizations as diverse as Wal-Mart and Nordstrom (where these people are called concierges). Both of these retailers pride themselves on having their people "own the problem" by taking care of customers' needs personally until these needs are resolved. Ask where an item is and they take you by the hand and walk you to it. If they can't answer your questions, they will find someone who can.

Could your organization make your customers' experience at the point of reception better? After all, that is where their first impressions are formed. And please, don't call it a "waiting room"!

# #98 Let's Get Personal

The first place that I introduced this idea was in a medical practice, but with today's technology, anyone can and should be doing it. One of the areas of patient care that is most lacking today is what used to be called the "bedside manner." That was back in the days when doctors made house calls; they knew you, they knew your family, and they had cared for generations of your family tree, at their bedside.

Today, because of the high-tech, low-touch nature of business, the importance and impact of relationship building is even more critical. You must start getting to know your customers (and patients) as real people with real lives, not just as customers with money or an insurance card.

I will never forget going into a new restaurant in my former neighborhood (James Street Restaurant in Pittsburgh, PA), and as many of us do, I asked for a particular booth. Many times I was meeting with a client or new prospect and just wanted a little privacy and comfort.

After my second or third visit, I had made a lunchtime reservation and was running a little late that day. I got to James Street about fifteen to twenty minutes late and was greeted at the door by the proprietor, Craig. He said, "John! We've been expecting you. We're holding your booth for you." I didn't know I had my own booth! Not only did that make a lasting impression on me, but it was also a nice touch with my client prospect.

That was quite a few years ago, and I have since moved away, but I continue to find a way to return to James Street Restaurant whenever I can, and I continue to tell this story to others because such a simple gesture can make all the difference between being just another customer or being someone special.

An easy way to do this is to start keeping notes on the personal information that customers share with you. In a medical practice, it is as simple as writing down the relevant small talk, such as vacation plans, hobbies, or other personal information, in the chart so that the next time you see this patient, you can prompt yourself to ask, "How was Aruba?" "How's the grandson?" "How's that new car running?" You get the idea.

Even if patients don't share such information, you already have their date of birth and other demographic information, so make a note to wish them a happy birthday if you happen to be seeing them around that time. Better yet, send them a card even if you don't see them!

Also, if you pay attention to your patients' hobbies and other interests, and you happen to run across an article, brochure, event, or any other item that may be of interest to them, jot a note on the corner and drop it in the mail. Yes, I said mail (not e-mail or fax). Some things are better done the old-fashioned way; especially if it shows extra effort and personalization. Snail mail stands out because it has less to compete with than e-mail does today; and it can be thrown in a briefcase and taken home.

This is where today's technology can really help you out. There's a slew of contact management software out there, making it a no-brainer to reinforce your customer relationships by entering this type of information into your customer database and letting the computer remind you and even automatically generate a letter or a card for you. All you have to do is send it out. And, as is the case with many of the ideas in this book, this one can be extended to include employees, their families, prospects, or anyone else in your circle of influence.

# #99 Waste Not, Want Not

As you have probably learned by now, food and beverage is a catalyst to all things good. And, as a professional speaker and trainer, I have had more than my share of free buffets, continental breakfasts, and other grub as part of training programs, meetings, and special events. Have you ever thought about what happens to the leftovers? Few people do.

Most times they are either thrown out or scavenged by attendees and taken back to various departments for later munching, after which they are thrown out anyway. I am always amazed at people's response when I suggest that we take leftovers to a local homeless shelter or food bank. Never once has anyone objected. People are usually just surprised that they hadn't thought of it before.

I have even volunteered to take them myself, if someone just wraps and boxes them up for me. In fact, in one cold, wintry Midwestern city where I could find no homeless shelters nearby, I just drove down the city streets and handed sandwiches out my car window to homeless people on my way back to the hotel room.

Some organizations have expressed some reluctance to do this because they are afraid of potential liability issues. Call me a risk taker, but I am willing to take that chance. I have yet to have a hungry, homeless person sue me over a bad sandwich. Some cities have organizations that actually come around to collect restaurants' unused, unserved food and have blanket liability insurance just in case.

Beyond leftovers, you can do a similar thing with your own products that may be overruns, irregulars, or outdated. It doesn't have to be limited to rejects, or to food, to be a win-win. For example, the optical retail chain LensCrafters operates a "Gift of Sight" charitable program to provide eyeglasses for children whose families cannot afford them. This is great public relations as well as a great social good. Take a look around your company and see what you have that may be either unneeded, underused, or better donated to someone else.

"Waste Not, Want Not" is a simple, effortless way to share your abundance while showing the world what you really stand for.

# #100 Get a Life

Let's assume that you have read this far and have come to the realization that your company just doesn't do a very good job at any of the stuff in this book. And let's assume that you don't see a lot of hope that they ever will. And for whatever reason, let's assume that you still want to work there. Are you nuts?

Okay, so maybe you are close to some magic milestone (like vesting in the savings plan), or your family and personal situation requires you to stay put, or you just don't have the authority to do these things (yet!). Whatever the reason, there is still hope for you personally to improve your lot in work and life. You may not be able to change your company, but you *can* enhance your own satisfaction with the world of work in which you live.

In the good old days it was called "moonlighting." People had to sneak around if they wanted to work a second job. It was usually done in the dark of night and had to be kept secret. And it was almost always done purely for the extra income, just to make ends meet. It wasn't intended to be fun. It was necessary.

Today, it is called a "composite career," and the reasons and conditions are quite different. Given that we have evolved from a muscle to a mental workforce, a brawn to a brain economy, people need to tend to their mental health and wellbeing more than ever, which is leading to the development and promotion of *avocations* in addition to our traditional *occupations*.

Whether you are looking for a way to use the other half of your brain (also see "Talent Show"), an avenue to release your other talents on the world, or you just want to find a more fun place to be, you can still "Get a Life," and more and more people are doing it. For example, my accountant is also an actor in local theater. I play in a classic rock garage band with a bunch of other frustrated old hippies who also have real jobs. My financial planner does television spots on cable news TV and even appeared in a major soap opera when it was filming in our town. I had a friend at the IRS (if that is possible) who tended bar on the weekends. I am sure you know someone first-hand who has found a nonwork diversion that could also be considered another job.

Although money could be the motivator, most high-performance workers take on these extracurricular avocations primarily for their mental health and the stimulation they provide. Getting paid is just the icing on the cake. If you work in a highly technical field (like financial planning or working for the IRS), it may be relaxing to do something a little more creative and a little more fun (like acting or bartending). Or, if you have a rather brainless job, you may want to take on a more cerebral extracurricular activity. You decide what rounds you out and just do it.

One participant in my Tapping Your Natural Weirdness program wrote to me four years later to tell me about her "weird" husband. After working for twenty-five years in corporate America (DuPont, Dow, Bayer), he purchased a luxury, converted forty-foot MCI bus and advertised that he would take up to four nice people anywhere in the United States, Canada, Mexico, and, eventually, South America at any time. This was not a conventional tour-bus trip going from point A to point B. It was so out-of-the-box that the Public Utilities Commission (which regulates and approves such things) classified his private motor coach as experimental.

So regardless how many of the ideas you use from this book at your current company, you can still Get Weird! in your own world of work. Just think about what you would "like" to do as opposed to what you "have" to do, and you may even make some extra cash in the process. Who knows, you may even retire in order to do what really makes you happy! When your work is no longer work, you have attained the ultimate state of weirdness.

# WHERE'S #101?

## (aka IT'S ALL IN YOUR HEAD!)

*You've already got it, I hope! If you've read this far and still haven't come up with an original thought, please call 911. In fact, never mind—you're already brain-dead! For all the rest of you, this is your opportunity to realize the difference between creativity and innovation. You may recall from the introduction to Part 1 that a key difference between creativity and innovation is implementation, i.e., doing something with your idea(s).*

*Go back to your "Personal Brainspurt Journal" and see which ideas you think are your real gems. Okay, I'll even accept some diamonds in the rough. Now, complete the enclosed form and either fax it or e-mail it to me. If any of your ideas qualify as truly weird (that's a good thing, remember?) and make it into the next manuscript I submit for publication, I'll send you, free, an autographed copy of* Get Weird! *to pass on to a friend or colleague—not to mention the legacy of weirdness you'll be leaving. One idea = one book: Now that's pay for performance! I told you this book would prove to be a great return on your investment. And that doesn't even count all the money you've already saved on conferences and seminars, where people are usually happy to get just one or two ideas.*

*So, welcome to the Wonderful World of Weirdness. Now, get weird and go out and do something new!*

### *Hey, Wizard of Weirdness!*
### *I've Got an Idea!*

Here's my idea: _____

_____

_____

_____

_____

_____

_____

_____

_____

_____

_____

(use separate page if necessary)

My name is: _____

My employer is: _____

My address is: _____

_____

My e-mail is: _____

**Send this form to:**
John Putzier, FirStep, Inc.
One Prospect Place, 223 Oakview Drive
Prospect, PA 16052-3147
Fax: 724-865-2800
E-mail: john@getweird.net
Web site: www.getweird.net

*Got something to say? For a good time, call John Putzier toll free at*
*1-866 GET WEIRD*

# Alphabetical List of Ideas

# Organizations Noted in the Text

# ABOUT THE AUTHOR

John Putzier is President of FirStep, Inc., and an adjunct faculty member of Carnegie Mellon University's H. John Heinz III Graduate School of Public Policy and Management. A prolific author and accomplished speaker, trainer, and consultant, Putzier brings a powerful blend of experience, education, and results to clients in search of innovative workplace initiatives. Past and present clients include 3M, Pepsi, FUJI, SmithKline Beecham, and a host of high-tech companies, among many others. Putzier is also a well-respected source of commentary, highly regarded for his expertise in current workplace issues and trends by such publications as *The Washington Post, Business Week, Inc.*, and *HR Magazine*.

He is the founder and past president of the Society for Human Resource Management High-Tech-Net, which now boasts thousands of members worldwide. And he is a lifetime-certified Senior Professional in Human Resources (SPHR), an honor bestowed by the Society for Human Resource Management's Certification Institute.

Mr. Putzier also founded and served as president of the Pennsylvania Speakers Association, a chapter of the National Speakers Association. He received his Bachelor of Science in Industrial Psychology from the University of Akron and holds a Master of Science in Human Resource Development from the American University in Washington, D. C.